TEXAS COLLEGE GUIDE

THE UNIVERSITY OF TEXAS AT AUSTIN

FIRST EDITION

BY JESSICA GIVENS

TEXAS COLLEGE GUIDE

THE UNIVERSITY OF TEXAS AT AUSTIN

By Jessica Givens

All-in-One Academics, a DBA of

SJG Professional Communications, Inc.

1129 W Pierce

Houston, TX 77019

www.allinoneacademics.com

ISBN 978-0-9903702-0-8

Printed in the United States of America

Cover Design: Jill Ort Haskell

Interior Design: Jill Ort Haskell

Cover Image: www.gettyimages.com

Back Cover Photo by Jill Hunter, courtesy of The Scout Guide

First Edition: May 2014

TABLE OF CONTENTS

FOREWORD

During the summer of 2013, it occurred to me that I should write down everything I knew about UT, plus everything I could dig up that seemed immediately relevant to the people I knew craved information. I certainly underestimated the scope of the project!

In this book, you will find an assessment of the different majors at UT, an approach to the UT application, and an interpretation of current data – all with a personal spin. In every instance possible, I have informally queried or spoken with various persons at the University of Texas in the know, and I have literally sifted through hundreds of the University's pages. Many of the descriptions of majors include paraphrases of individual pages on the UT website.

Throughout the different major and career discussions, you will find various salary data. Except for the few that are noted otherwise, all information came directly from the Bureau of Labor Statistics webpage, a site that is regularly updated by the United States Department of Labor. I grew tired of citing it every time, so I eventually stopped. However, I want to say that we are so lucky that our government keeps such records; they are incredibly helpful!

I have to say a few quick words of thanks. First, my husband and my parents are amazing pillars of support. Without my husband, Jamil Driscoll, I would fall to pieces; he is my perfect partner in everything from business to travel to CrossFit. My mother is largely responsible for this book's existence because she painstakingly edited each page, and I know she will promote it shamelessly to anyone who will listen. She's the most incredible person I know. My father has been my academic inspiration; were it not for his vision, I might not have understood the value of pursuing a passion. He was the first person who ever told me to do what I really loved, and he provided me with the cushy foundation to make academic choices that probably seemed impractical at first glance. Second, I have to say thank you to Rachelle Bart because she's the reason this business exists. I would have gone into the poor house long ago without her. Third, my students – B John, Drew, Pace, Lacy, Kat, Sassy, Daren, Walter, Austin, Blayne, Pia, Morgan, Kienne, Creed, Brittany, Chris, Ale, Lizzie, Emma, Rachael, Walker, Peyton, Mary Elizabeth, and so many others – have given me strength and made me want to always do my best, lest I let any one of them down.

INTRODUCTION

When I applied to college in 1995, getting into the University of Texas was pretty much a given. After all, I had high SAT scores and good grades. That's all you needed...well, that plus a completed application before the deadline. When I started working with students in 1999 on SAT preparation for the Princeton Review, I think the situation was relatively the same: Good kids got into UT Austin because they showed promise, even if they weren't valedictorians or National Merit Scholars. However, just two years later, I got a minor introduction to the growing fears about UT admissions. In 2001, I helped a student – let's call him Corby – with his test prep, and he was seriously concerned about getting rejected from UT Austin. Honestly, I thought he was nuts, but I went through the motions. His score went up from a 970 to a 1210 (that was before the addition of the writing section, and the test was just out of 1600, so this was a HUGE improvement) – but we aren't here to talk about test prep prowess. (In fact, I despise test preparation, although it constitutes a large part of my tutoring company's business, filling the void as a necessary evil.) Anyway, what matters is that Corby got into UT with that 1210, even though he was ranked in probably the 3rd quarter at Stratford High School, a competitive Houston school. At the time, I felt validated, as though my initial dismissal of rising standards at UT Austin had been correct. I might have started to see some conflicting evidence even at that time, but shortly thereafter, the Twin Towers fell and my attention was diverted, as was everyone else's.

However, I got a rude awakening in 2005 when my student Blake applied to University of Texas. Blake had a 27 on the ACT, was in the top quarter at Memorial High School, had completed hundreds of service hours, had won national competitions in Business Professionals of America, held leadership positions in virtually every organization to which he belonged (of which there were many), and clearly demonstrated the potential to excel in the arena of business. When he got his rejection letter, I was flummoxed. How could the situation have changed so drastically? I could barely process what I saw as a complete injustice. I wanted to understand what had gone wrong, so I started to read.

I began by researching the admissions policies at the University of Texas, and at that time, they offered automatic admission to the top ten percent of Texas high schools. Stories told of people starting to change high schools, moving to less competitive options in order to improve their class rank. It seemed a little out-of-control, to be perfectly frank.

I also started to read about the varying competition in different majors at UT and came to understand that not all majors were created equal in their admissions considerations. Since I attended a small liberal arts college that allowed people to change majors freely and didn't require students to declare a major until their junior year, the concept didn't immediately compute for me, and it also took quite a while for it to compute to the parents whose children I helped, too. It was a new system, one that had not quite prepared itself for applicant dishonesty and one that was ready to be exploited. As the criteria for automatic admissions has gotten tougher – changing to only top 8% in 2012 and to top 7% in 2013! –attempts to game the system have become commonplace.[1]

Let me explain the ramifications of the system in the recent past: A student with mediocre numbers overall could apply to the College of Education and be accepted, while a student very near the top of his or her class with outstanding test scores could apply to the Cockrell School of Engineering get the thumbs-down sign. For many people, the major-selection game because a tremendous part of the process, as people attempted to jack with the system and look for overlooked areas of study that might yield easier admission. In truth, it really worked for quite some time, and to some degree it works today, but what's interesting is that the standards have risen so substantially in all areas that it doesn't suffice just to put down a phony major anymore. It's more about assessing a student's interests and building an application that best showcases how that student's experiences demonstrate sincere passion and corroborate his or her choice of a major at the University of Texas at Austin.

After years of working with students and achieving a very high success rate of helping students gain admission to UT Austin, I have seen that a proven track record of involvement and focus in a given area can provide students with a real edge in admission to UT, and I've really had it with deception and subterfuge. UT applicants – you or your kids or your grandkids – are real people with meaningful histories and experiences that merit an honest and comprehensive display. However, you also deserve to understand what makes an applicant competitive for a given major, so that you don't waste your major selection on choices that are absurd long shots. Next, you need to understand how the majors are different, what types of careers they cultivate, and what sorts of job and income prospects you'll have after graduation. Finally, you need to know the other options that exist for paving a pathway to the University of Texas at Austin, because a rejection letter as an incoming freshman is not the end of the world, nor is it the end of the story. And, that's why I've written this book, to give you the information you need and to prevent you from falling victim to shysters in this dodgy day and age of admissions chicanery. Additionally, I've fact-checked every aspect of my work with the University of Texas, combing their website for content and keeping in close contact with admissions and various UT departments. This book is a one-stop reference for UT major selection and admissions. Yes, it's a very narrow book because it deals with only one university, but UT is the largest university around, so why not give it some solo attention?

1

UT ADMISSIONS PRACTICES

Because the University of Texas has so many qualified applicants, the University has had to find a way to evaluate applicants fairly. As a result, the school has come up with a method that mimics the graduate application model. Essentially, you apply to the school that best suits your interests, and you make a case for your acceptance. UT is looking for future Texas graduates, people who want to graduate in a field of study, not people who want to fudge their experiences to get into the school.

Academic Fit

In its admissions process the University is clearly trying to match students to their academic fit. To stand out against the crush of applicants, a student has to demonstrate that he or she is attempting to be the best at his or her chosen field. If you select a science major, you need to demonstrate an aptitude for science, as well as the tenacity to stick it out during the grueling parts of the program. This is where your transcript and résumé really come into play – have you shown verifiable talent and interest?

Scoring a File

There is (and there can be) no set standard. The process of admissions at UT is fluid, and it changes on a yearly basis. What's most important for you to know is that the different components of your application are scored – and not always by the same person.

Major Selection

Once you submit your application, it gets parked at your first-choice major. While a few of our students have gotten their second choice majors, the vast majority have not. That's because UT has mainly considered the first-choice major. This means something extremely significant to you as an applicant: You need to put the best information you have together to create a solid case for your first-choice major. If there's any way to tie in a second-choice in your essay C, then by all means, do so, but understand that your first choice is going to be the one that gets the greatest consideration.

Many students put engineering because it's their dream major, but they haven't really built the profile to earn a position in such a competitive program. – perhaps they haven't gone through Calculus or taken an AP science course in school… As a result, they get passed over in the UT admissions process, and they wonder why. Well, it's because interest does not equate to merit or preparation. You have to challenge yourself to go above and beyond, proving that you not only want to get into UT in a certain field; you also want to graduate in that field.

You might wonder why UT wants such young people to make such critical life decisions. Well, the school prides itself on intense pre-professional sequences in most programs. Additionally, the University wants to get its students in and out with as little debt as possible – which means you can't stay in school forever! You need to drill down to your interests early, therefore, and assert your preferences from the start of your college career. Sure, people do hop around in their majors once they enroll at UT, but the University wants to minimize the hopping.

Looking for Loopholes

Everyone asks, "What's the easiest way to get into UT?" They hope to camouflage themselves to fit a less competitive major, so that they can circumvent the rigorous selection process at UT. I can't say that I necessarily fault people for thinking this way; after all, the "closet major" strategy worked for years. However, now, too many people have gotten wind of the concept.

Recent attempts to game the admissions system often backfire because so many people have jumped on the bandwagon. People thought education was an easy major, so a zillion people applied to education. All of a sudden, education became swamped with applicants, and obviously, the competition to get into education soared. Simultaneously, other majors received fewer applications and became less competitive. That meant that qualified students got rejected from UT because they applied to the major they thought would be least competitive. If they had just applied for the major that interested them, they might have gotten in. Your takeaway from this should be that it doesn't make sense to waste valuable time playing a guessing game about which majors will be less or more sought-after in a given year; you need to use that time to assess and capitalize on your own strengths.

That brings us to a difficult question, however. What do you do if your real passion is business or engineering, but you're not at the top of your class? I would look at your next best strength and apply through that program, whether it's in the natural sciences, liberal arts, etc. UT admissions would probably kill me for supporting that course of action because it's more focused on getting into UT than it is on graduating from UT, but I understand that no one wants a rejection letter. You might get one from UT no matter which major you choose, but the chances are higher with engineering or business. Do with that information what you will. You cannot make up experiences – if you try, they will sound inauthentic and shallow. Pick a major that does truly interest you, something that aligns with your passions and talents. Don't try to outsmart the admissions committee; they've looked at thousands (probably tens of thousands) of applications, so they're a step ahead at all times.

Undecided

It's time address a real issue that often goes ignored: Some high school students just haven't got their futures totally figured out! Oh, the horrors! You mean to tell me that an eighteen year old might feel some indecision in this world where options seem to multiply by the second? Yeah, I get it, and UT does, too.

The School of Undergraduate Studies (UGS) is a beautiful, safe holding ground for freshman and sophomore students who are trying to decide which field best suits their talents and career goals. Students can stay classified as students of UGS for up to four semesters, but the majority of students pick their UT degree-granting college by the second or third semester of school.

In applying to the School of Undergraduate Studies, you would just want to be honest on your Essay C. Explain that you are passionate about learning but that you have yet to set your career plans into stone. It's okay to be undecided!

To AP or Not to AP?

One of my greatest interests at the outset was to assess the relative value of AP courses. I was exceptionally curious because my public school students had so many more AP courses than my private school students. In fact, some of my private school students had been discouraged from taking AP courses because their advisors prioritized getting an A over taking the more rigorous course. That didn't make any sense to me because colleges need to see that a student is capable of hacking it in the most challenging courses. Furthermore, AP courses provide students with a more in-depth foundation to take into their college classes.

The simple fact is that UT values academic achievement. The University is looking for students who push themselves, but a student doesn't have to take every available AP to be competitive for admission. (You still might need to take all AP's to qualify for the top 7% at your school.) Instead, you should be strategic in your AP course selection. If you are passionate about pursuing a career in engineering, you should consider taking AP Calculus and AP Physics, but if you're not a history wizard, then maybe you could take an on-level history class.

Under any circumstances, you need to understand that AP credits, while useful, can sometimes work against you. Why? Because you might place out of some lower-level courses at UT and find yourself in exceedingly challenging advanced classes. I don't want your GPA to suffer like that. Therefore, I encourage you to take your basic courses again. For instance, don't skip out of Calculus I only to struggle through Calculus II. Take Calculus I in college and get an A. Then, soar through Calculus II.

Therefore, overall, when determining your course lineup in high school, I encourage you to take AP classes in the areas that most correlate with your intended major. For example, if you want to study journalism, you should take AP English and perhaps AP History. If you want to study chemistry, then take AP Chemistry and AP Calculus, as well as honors courses in the other sciences. Be strategic in your selections because you want to make good grades. Like so many aspects of life, your choice of AP classes is about quality, not quantity.

Using Your Local Community College

You probably already know this, but I'll say it anyway – just in case you haven't fully appreciated your reality. Texas is awesome. Our colleges are incredible, and they want to help their students graduate with as little debt as possible. The University of Texas prides itself on helping its students graduate in as little time as possible, and the Universiwty has stated increasing the four-year graduation rate as one of its explicit missions.[2] Consequently, UT often smiles upon students who have earned college credit before starting at the University. There are two main ways to get college credit before enrolling in a university: dual credit and concurrent enrollment.

Dual Credit is an articulated program between a high school and a community college. I remember that my AP U.S. History class was the first one in our district to earn credit at a community college. It seemed like a no-brainer at the time, something so small and insignificant. Little did I know, I was participating in the start of an exciting new set of academic opportunities. Eighteen years out from my initial Houston Community College dual credit course, my students are now enrolled in multiple dual credit courses, using their time in high school to minimize their work in college. Many of my students have used dual credit to work through at least 12 hours, and the highly motivated ones have completed upwards of 18. While I have never sat on the other end of the application's "Submit" button, I imagine that good grades in those classes can only enhance a candidate's profile. After all, A's and B's in those courses show an ability to handle accredited, college-level material, and they put student a step ahead when they start at UT with regard to credit hours. My private school students rarely have that cushion because only a few private schools have negotiated a dual-credit agreement with local community colleges.

However, there are other ways to get community college during high school than through dual credit. You can also do what's called concurrent enrollment, which means that you will have to become a student at your local community college; you would take classes directly through the community college and would not earn high school credit for them. The reality is that this can sometimes be a better option. You can take classes over the summer or in the evening, or you can probably even sign up to do some of them online.

Now, you might be inspired; why not do a jillion classes and square away as many hours as possible? I used to feel the same way! However, I now realize the importance of being cautious in venturing into concurrent enrollment AND/OR dual credit. Your grades in those courses can positively or negatively affect you in college. Say that you start UT in the School of Undergraduate Studies with the goal of transferring into the McCombs School of Business. Well, when you apply, the school will consider your entire college GPA, and if you have C's, or even B's, in your community college courses, you might fall below their expectations. That means that you need to take these community college classes extremely seriously. You need to get A's. If you're distracted or overwhelmed by other responsibilities, then do not take courses that can negatively affect your opportunities in the future. As I see it, "There is good credit and bad credit." You cannot afford to have bad credit, and if you do poorly in your concurrent enrollment or dual credit courses, that's precisely what you'll have.

Now, on the bright side, if you do well in your community college courses, UT will happily accept that transcript. It is not required to send your community college transcript for freshman admission, but good grades can positively affect your chances of admission. So, if you've done well, send your transcripts and discuss in an essay why you took those classes. It requires extra dedication and focus to excel simultaneously in community college classes and high school classes, so describe how it was worth tackling an unusually large workload to take another step towards your goals.

2

THE COCKRELL SCHOOL OF ENGINEERING

Engineering has always been hard. Even my Uncle John, now almost 74 years old, looks back at his engineering science and math courses and remembers them as grueling; it's simply a pain that doesn't fade with age. However, despite the misery of the course load, engineering is one of the most highly sought-after degrees in Texas – and, actually, in the world. If you look around at the objects in your midst – airplanes, computers, hypodermic needles, car engines, even sneakers – you are seeing evidence of engineering. Engineers learn how to make things that work, how to channel theoretical science into invention, and how to improve efficiency in business and everyday life. In Texas, engineering is a degree with a fabulous job outlook for the future, and I say Texas specifically because Texas is the home of unbelievable innovation in multiple industries. Oil companies, medical complexes, computing firms, and construction businesses all need engineers, and that need will continue to grow as Texas industry marches forward with its expansion. You might wonder whether Texas can sustain this growth in engineering-related industries, if only because what goes up often comes back down; however, Texas has offered industry a safe haven in many different ways. Texas is an inexpensive place for such companies to operate because we have no state income tax and we offer incentives to new businesses for calling Texas home. Plus, we have a booming population and maintain probably the greatest enthusiasm and spirit of any state. While that could all come to a screeching halt, it seems unlikely.

If you have the aptitude to study engineering, I would do it, and here's why: Engineering is something you cannot go back and do later. You can always get an MBA or the prerequisites for medical school or a teaching certificate, but you need to do engineering as an undergraduate student. Studying engineering can only open your options for the future, but so few students have the drive to persevere in the field because of the difficulty I mentioned earlier. That said, I encourage you to suck it up.

Now, let's talk about the basic facts for getting into the UT Austin engineering school: In almost every engineering major it offers, UT is ranked among the top in the nation. You literally can't go wrong here – if you can get in. Many people are under the misconception that, by qualifying for automatic admission to UT through class rank, a student automatically can get into whatever major he or she wants. This is patently false. Automatic admission to UT Engineering simply does not happen because the school is so competitive.

So, what does it take to be admitted to UT's Cockrell School of Engineering?

Stated school requirements: Calculus readiness. See UT website for specific qualifications.[3]

Transcript: A student's course load in school should show an aptitude for math and science. For a future engineering student, it is important to take the highest available levels of math and science, including the hardest calculus classes and AP science courses – and you need to get A's. And, if there are engineering courses a student can take at school, perhaps as part of a technical education curriculum, I highly recommend it. That adds depth to the application and reveals drive. There's no good reason for a budding engineer to take Psychology AP over Chemistry AP, nor should he or she take a fourth year of Spanish over an engineering course. Try to look at high school courses as preparation, not as requirements. The more math and science a student takes, the better his or her chances of success in the engineering course sequence.

Résumé: You really want to cultivate an interest in science and math. If a student can participate in science fairs or attend math competitions, that would be fantastic. You know, there are regional math competitions through UIL; you might want to check them out. Another great option is to get a summer internship at a firm that employs engineers in the field that interests you ("fields" are explained in greater detail below). Start by Googling that field and the name of a nearby city and start making phone calls to see if you can shadow an engineer or an engineering team for a few days over the summer. With respect to community service, see if you can do something that requires construction and hands-on work, like Habitat for Humanity or helping an elderly neighbor with home repairs. For future engineers, there are also cool summer programs at universities around Texas, all of which are searchable on the internet, and those can provide you with better insight into what interests you, too, making you better prepared to describe your goals and interests.

Test scores: A high math score on standardized testing will prove helpful. An 800 on the math section of the SAT will compensate for a weaker reading score (engineers aren't the best literary scholars, generally speaking).

DEGREE PROGRAMS IN ENGINEERING

1. Aerospace Engineering and Engineering Mechanics

You may never have heard of aerospace engineering, or you may associate it primarily with flying airplanes or sending astronauts into space. But, there's so much more to this area of study. While it definitely includes a study of space for the purpose of exploration, the purpose of the degree is to understand how to use our access to space to better understand Earth. Considering that I've worked with hundreds of students and not one of them has mentioned aerospace engineering, I believe this avenue to be potentially quite lucrative, and since the human race has learned to navigate the skies, our interest in developing aerospace technology has remained a steady force; therefore, you will probably have a lifetime of career opportunities with a degree in this field.

Median pay 2012: $103,720

Expected growth: ^7% (slower than average)[4]

2. Biomedical Engineering

Biomedical engineering has gotten more popular in recent years because of the tremendous breakthroughs we've all witnessed in the diagnosis and treatment of disease. Biomedical engineers are at the core of that exciting change, and given the fact that we can always improve our medical and health technology, biomedical engineers will always have a place in the workforce. In the Cockrell School, students can choose from three pathways: Biomedical Imaging and Instrumentation, Cellular and Biomolecular Engineering, or Computational Biomedical Engineering. This program is extremely competitive, with only 100 kids accepted each year, and for the lucky few who do make the cut, the atmosphere is nurturing and supportive. The department helps its students get great internships and gives students excellent research opportunities. This last year, CNN Money said that biomedical engineering was the number one job in America, and the job growth rate over the last ten years has been 61.7%![5] The moral of the story: you may have a hard time getting into the biomedical engineering program in the Cockrell School, but if you make the cut, you'll have a rewarding career ahead of you with great future prospects.

Median pay 2012: $86,960

Expected growth: ^27% (much faster than average)

3. Chemical Engineering

This is one of the most popular, most traditional fields of engineering, and it's one of the first fields kids usually consider when they're looking into engineering, initially because they've heard of it and then because chemical engineering provides such a broad base. Chemical engineers can literally work in almost in any field. At UT, chemical engineering undergrads work hand-in-hand with researchers, so Chem E students at UT can look forward to solid job prospects. So, while the rest of the world is in a state of economic contraction, chemical engineering is trekking right along! What's important to know is that the school took fewer than 150 students as incoming chemical engineering freshmen this year.[6] That means it's highly competitive, which makes sense, right?

2012 Median pay: $94,350

Expected growth: ^4% (slower than average)[7]

4. Civil And Architectural Engineering

Civil engineering is a classical line of study within the field of engineering, and if you look around you – down at the roads that map the routes of our lives, out at the waterways that bring us clean drinking water and minimize flooding, and towards the transportation systems that move people to and from the activities in their lives – all of that, and more, is overseen by civil engineers. There are actually multiple formal areas of practice within civil engineering, but the most important concept to grasp is that civil engineers work to improve daily life.[8] Every pathway offers different work environments, different pay scales, and different future prospects.

The second line of study, architectural engineering, is more about structures and the materials and processes that allow for their creation. If you're a person who wants to influence the way people live in their everyday environments, one of these fields may be great for you. There is good job stability in these areas of engineering, but the pay is not as high as in other areas. Still, it's quite respectable by comparison to other fields, and life is about striving for happiness and comfort. Although I haven't known any architectural engineers, I've known many happy civil engineers. This may be a great area for you if you're into the career options you find on the UT website.

Median salary in 2012: $79,340

Predicted job growth: ^20% (about average)

5. Electrical And Computer Engineering

At UT, electrical and computer engineering are lumped together within the same program for the first two years because they have so many core studies in common. When a student hits junior year, he or she will have to pick a path and specialize. The early marriage of electrical and computer engineering at UT is extremely useful to UT students because of the extensive overlap in the two fields. Now, let's look at them in a little more detail:

Electrical: I'll be honest and say that I know very little about electrical engineering. I started researching it because I wanted to help guide students who showed an interest in tinkering with computers and electronics. What I've found in my research has really blown me away. Did you know that at UT there's actually a group working on making an invisibility cloak???[9] That very concept is mindboggling, and it's evidence of how incredible this program is. The program is also deeply connected with industry, so that its students have tremendous opportunities for employment after graduation. What do electrical engineers do? They basically work on everything electrical, meaning motors, communications, navigation, power, etc. Any electronic object that plays a part in your life probably spent a great deal of time with an electrical engineer (or 100 different electrical engineers) before it went to market.

Computer: Computer engineers also work in the field of electricity, but usually in the area of circuits and motherboards, etc. They develop the little chips that rule our lives, and they will continue to have an impact on the world. However, it's important to note that computer hardware has ceased to be the chief area of development; the world is moving more towards software improvement and innovation. That's why the job growth is lower than you might have imagined. If you want to create software and work in the brainy realm of programming, you might be better served redirecting your interest toward computer science. That said, we will always want new devices, and there will never be an end to the human desire to build and create. As a computer engineer, you can be at the forefront of robotics and nanocomputers, so if that's what you're into, by all means press forward.

Electrical engineers

Median pay 2012: $89,630

Expected job growth: ^4% (slower than the average)

Computer engineers

Median pay 2010: $100,920

Expected job growth: ^7% (slower than the average)

6. Mechanical Engineering

Mechanical engineering is one of those trusty standby degrees; it's broad and flexible, and it's here to stay. Mechanical engineering prepares you to design and test machinery of all types. At some schools, that might not sound so exciting, but at UT Austin, there are so any different areas of study, from nanoengineering to nuclear engineering. The fact is, you have such incredible faculty with such diverse research interests that you can zero in on what it is that fascinates you. Unlike many schools, UT has the resources to nurture and further those interests. It's important with mechanical engineering to think long-term because the mechanical engineers who have the greatest opportunities for success are those who are well informed about new technology. If you're interested in an evolving career, mechanical engineering may be for you, but if you aren't willing to continue learning for the rest of your life, this may not be your best option. Mechanical engineering is so useful in so many different industries that the degree has the potential to endure, despite ups and downs in individual markets. A mechanical engineer can transition from one field to another because of his or her broadly applicable education. I wish all degrees offered that stability. To me, it sounds pretty great.

We encourage you to check out the vast number of specialties for mechanical engineers on the UT website.

Median pay 2013: $84,770

Expected job growth: ^9% (slower than the average)

7. Petroleum Engineering

This is the field for Texas, as most people know, and UT Austin has consistently held one of the top two positions for petroleum engineering. I'm not usually one for ranks because I think there are so many factors, but in Texas, what you can't take away from us is our history in the petroleum industry; I think it's only fair that our universities are at the top! It's important to know that the Petroleum and Geosystems Engineering program at UT is small, with only 93 students admitted in fall 2012, and the SAT scores and class rank were near the very top.[10] I have had students accepted to the program who weren't within those ranges, but they were kids who showed real promise in the field of Petroleum Engineering. If you're interested in this program, I suggest you start thinking early about how you can learn more about the field.

I want to add a quick personal note to this particular major. I once listened to one of my students in a conversation with his dad about going into the oil industry. The father had been extremely successful in a business that negotiated the sale of oil rigs, but his son remained unconvinced that the business would prove similarly lucrative for him because everything he had heard in school said that oil was running out. How could he make money in an industry that was depleting its only resource? The father responded in a way that both amused and astounded me. He said, "You're right, Pace. When you're my age, there won't be any more oil for $100 a barrel, but there will be plenty at $400 a barrel." His point: Oil will be here to stay (with rising prices) until we've used the very last drop. ***My point:*** Petroleum engineers will probably have jobs for a long time to come.

On a practical level of actually getting into the UT program, it's going to be tough. This is without a doubt one of the most sought-after degrees in the United States right now, simply because oil appears to be a never-ending fountain of wealth. And, the truth is that, as long as oil prices continue to rise (a situation that really depends more on OPEC than on anything else), oil companies will have the money to invest in new technologies. That means that petroleum engineers have positive prospects for the foreseeable future. Yes, it is true that in the past oil prices have plummeted, and petroleum engineers have experienced a level of job insecurity. Still, the risks are small, and the rewards are great. This is a practical, good field that can provide limitless career options. However, it is important to note that there are NOT many spots in the petroleum engineering program at UT, and you may have to look elsewhere if this is the major of your dreams.

Median pay 2012: $130,280

Expected job growth: ^26% (much faster than average)

3

THE MOODY COLLEGE OF COMMUNICATION

The Moody College of Communication is especially attractive to people who are interested in media, want to study methods of communication, or want to apply creative skills to a practical profession. Communications is a broad discipline, and people who major in communications of some type can go on to do almost anything. That's one reason the school has become increasingly competitive for admission: the areas of study often include clear career preparation, an appealing consideration in a time of economic uncertainty. While some schools may offer a broad "communication" degree, UT is special because it has the resources to help students diversify and find their niche. Unlike the College of Engineering, the College of Communication has a more forgiving approach to math and sciences: You don't have to compute the launch angle of a projectile in order to brand an emerging tennis shoe company, but you do have to write and speak well. Therefore, the College of Communication appeals to students who are clever and creative, but not necessarily math and science whizzes.

At UT, one other attractive aspect of the College of Communication is the well-developed set of enrichment programs. From the Semester in Los Angeles, where UT has its own center in Burbank, to a photojournalism Maymester in the Czech Republic to the highly practical Business Foundations Certificate through the McCombs School, UT has had the resources, time, and energy to build a program that could meet anyone's interests. It's worth spending an hour or so on their website to see greater details because I could literally go on for pages about this and still not touch on every point.

Now, how can you build a résumé that's attractive to the College of Communication? If you're passionate about communication, I encourage you to start getting involved now in your high school's communication-related activities. You can sign up for Newspaper or Yearbook, or maybe your school has a small film program. One of my students, Nicole, was determined to work in film, but her school had no film department or film-related extracurricular activities. She showed innovation by using a home video camera to make movies with her friends and by starting a small, student-hosted film festival at her school in a classroom. Her peers brought in their reels, and they all played them for their friends and the faculty. Did she win any awards?

No, but she demonstrated an active commitment to working on film. She also signed up for a small, inexpensive film program at the University of Houston, which offers scholarships to promising students. Guess what? She got an acceptance letter to the RTF program at UT in December! (Please note, she was also an excellent student with a 30+ ACT score... so that definitely helped, but it didn't do the trick alone. She was NOT automatic.)

Another student, Carly, showcased her passion for writing by starting a blog where she made regular posts and by submitting articles to her school paper and literary magazine. She eventually became an editor for her paper, as well. Because of her depth of experience, when she applied to journalism, her interest in the major was clear.

You can follow in the footsteps of one of my students above, or you can do something different. For example, some schools offer broadcast journalism programs, during which students film a weekly news show for their peers to watch during homeroom. If your school doesn't, you could get a group of friends together and make a school news program that you put on YouTube for your peers to watch. If you're interested in working on communications disorders, volunteer with an organization that works with people who are struggling to overcome those issues. Despite the variations in these fields, people in Communications tend to be feisty and outgoing, so be bold and leave your comfort zone. Be sure to include everything you do on your résumé.

Let's take a look at the options. Just as a side note, I'm breaking it up by bigger departments and then drilling down into the possible focus areas.

1. ADVERTISING AND PUBLIC RELATIONS

Every time you get a popup on your computer and every time Pandora takes a break to bring you news from a sponsor, advertising is making its way into your life. In our consumer society, we are bombarded by company messages, encouraging us to buy a Mac not a PC and convincing us that if we just ate a bowl of Wheaties in the morning, we could all be as fit as Peyton Manning. While we recognize that ads play a role in our everyday lives, many of us fail to realize how important advertising is to big companies; it's NEVER going away. That's why people in advertising will always have a purpose. That said, advertising majors need to be creative and tireless, prepared to throw out a million different ideas to reach a perfect platform to pitch the value of a company's product. This is the field for someone who can think in terms of images and words because advertising is about stimulating the mind and spurring people into action.

Public relations is a similar field, but the purpose of public relations is to work on building a company's or a person's image. Public relations specialists write press releases to share positive news or to help clear the air after negative publicity. Public relations professionals need to be outgoing, always ready to introduce themselves to strangers and promote their agenda. PR is heavily dependent upon writing, so if you're interested in pursuing perfect grammar and witty phrasing, this may be the perfect profession for you.

With respect to a future in PR and Advertising, your internships and activities throughout college are of the utmost importance when you want to work in advertising and/or public relations. You don't have to work for a fancy company or get a paid internships to make waves; you DO need to get started with local companies, however. Volunteer your services for a budding business you like and support by designing their fliers or by helping with social media efforts. You can also help them pitch stories to local news outlets or work on coordinating a blog that gets noticed. One way or another, the more engaged and tenacious you are in your pursuits to build your resume early, the more likely you are to score a competitive, career-propelling internship for your UT requirement. And, no, a position in a sorority or fraternity won't cut the mustard. You need to leave the comforts of the familiar and show ingenuity because EVERYONE wants a cool job; don't you want to be the person to land one?

***Note:** In both advertising and public relations majors at UT, you will have a required internship to help you understand the field you have chosen firsthand and to give you work experience to enhance your chances of employment after graduation. You will have to submit a résumé for potential internship positions; it needs to have meat on it. Get started on small projects, like the ones I mentioned above, as early as your first semester of college!

Advertising and Marketing Managers

Median pay 2012 for advertising managers: $88,590

Median pay 2012 for marketing managers: $119,480

Expected job growth in both areas: ^12% (about the average)

Public Relations Specialists and Managers

Median pay 2012 for specialists: $54,170

Median pay 2012 for managers: $95,450

Expected job growth for specialists: ^12% (faster than the average)

Expected job growth for managers:^13% (about average)

2. COMMUNICATION SCIENCES AND DISORDERS

Communication at UT goes beyond helping people spread messages about business and building public images; it also includes a program that helps people overcome obstacles in communication. In this program, students select a specialization: audiology, speech-language pathology, or deaf education. All of these specialties offer students the option to go right out into the workforce and find jobs, either in private practice or large institutions, but your options will be broader if you go to grad school. Majors in Communication Sciences and Disorders have the capacity to make a meaningful difference in others' lives, a factor that can brighten even the most difficult day and make going to work worthwhile. In this field, UT encourages a great deal of student research, giving students the chance to work alongside professors, earn college credit, and build their résumés for graduate programs. Finally, in addition to the in-class requirements, students are required to complete a minimum of 25 hours of observation, which may be completed at the UT Speech and Hearing Center. It is important to note that you will probably have to go to graduate school if you hope to work in the fields of audiology or speech pathology. Don't let that fact discourage you because these are excellent career pathways, but just know what lies ahead.

Audiologist (after graduate degree)

Median pay 2012: $69,720

Expected job growth: ^34% (much faster than average)

Speech Pathologist (after graduate degree)

Median pay 2010: $69,870

Expected job growth: ^19% (faster than average)

3. JOURNALISM

Journalism is an interesting field to me because it is having to evolve with the times. As the Internet continues to redefine how people share information, journalism must take its cues, and the schools that breed journalists must figure out how to hone cutting edge skills in their students. UT has definitely taken the proverbial bull by the (long)horns here with the launch of its new journalism curriculum AND a new building, the Belo Center for New Media. Journalism at UT no longer means print; it's all about tearing down barriers. According to the school itself, "[they're] eliminating the old walls between print, magazine, photojournalism, multimedia and broadcast, and [they'll] be emphasizing good writing and critical thinking from Day One."[11] Here's why this is so important: there aren't as many reporting jobs as there once were, and journalists (in the traditional sense) aren't getting paid what they did in the past. Now, that said, a good journalist always has a keen eye for identifying ways to attract a reader's attention and for delivering a message.

Journalists may like writing news stories, but they have the skills to do a broad variety of jobs that involve effective writing and can become leaders in any industry. In fact, one of our most successful clients started out as a journalism major and found his way into the oil industry – only to emerge as CEO of an oilfield services company.

Another interesting, emerging field for people with strong writing skills is Technical Writing, which is basically the creation of quality manuals to accompany the zillions of products modern humans consume. A technical writer helps turn miserably complex content into digestible bits of information. The reason I mention this is that the field is growing, and there is no graduate degree requirement to become a technical writer. You might, however, complement your writing pursuits with some classes in computer science or web design – you could possibly even do it through some online courses at a community college or even a free open online course. In addition, there are certificates for advancement in technical writing through such organizations as the Society for Technical Communication and the American Medical Writers Association. Check those out to gain greater credentials without full-scale grad school.

Reporter or Correspondent

2012 Median Pay: $37,090

Job Outlook: ^13% (Yikes!)

Broadcast News Analyst

2012 Median Pay: $55,380

Job Outlook: ^13% (Yikes!)

Technical Writer

2012 Median Pay: $65,500

Expected Job Growth: ^15% (Faster than average)

4. COMMUNICATION STUDIES

At its most fundamental level, communication is the transmission of messages between two or more people, right? Well, some messages are delivered more effectively than others, and that's the reason for the Communication Studies department – to identify effective communication strategies and target them to specific disciplines within communications. ***There are three specialties within Communication Studies at UT:*** Corporate Communication, Human Relations, and Political Communication. We will look at each of these separately.

A. Corporate Communication:

Overall, corporate communication is a field of organizational communication that zeroes in on "communication between and among individuals and groups in organizations, including corporate, non-profit, and government organizations."[12] Corporate Communications Specialists often work within a larger organization to handle the communications that connect the people who are employed by the company; they write emails, put together newsletters, proofread communications, etc. The job description could vary tremendously, depending upon the company and the available position.

The Bureau of Labor and Statistics does not report the salary data of Corporate Communications specialists, but several websites weigh in on a rough average of $42,000.

B. Human Relations

Human relations involve interpersonal interactions, studying verbal and nonverbal communications. This field can translate into such jobs as Corporate Trainer, Labor Relations Consultant, Personnel Manager, etc.[13] While you don't necessarily need a master's degree to succeed in these areas, you will probably need to hone in on an area of interest and start to build a résumé in that direction, starting with your college internships.

Training and Development

2012 Median Pay: $95,400

Expected Job Growth: ^11% (about average)

Labor Relations Specialist

2012 Median Pay: $55,640

Expected Job Growth: ^7% (slower than average)

Personnel Manager (Human Resources)

2012 Median Pay: $99,720

Expected Job Growth: ^13%

C. Political Communication

This field deals with effective communication in the public setting. A person with a degree in this area would have the skills to work in politics or government, whether by working on campaigns or as speechwriters, lobbyists or government agents. Now, this may not be the field for everyone because it involves an intense study of political science and rhetoric (persuasive speaking). However, it's an area that is most definitely NOT going away, especially considering the increasing competitiveness and visibility of political campaigns and the escalating battles between corporations and Congress.

It is really hard to find salary data on these fields because people literally work for any salary between zero and seven figures – in fact, such political consultants as Karl Rove (conservative advising guru, who is a genius – regardless of one's political persuasions – but does not actually have a college degree) probably even exceed that number! Similarly, lobbyists are rewarded based on their experience and success rate. What is important is that you can enter this industry with only a bachelor's degree, and then you can see where your talents and interests lie. If you should at that point decide to go back for a master's or Ph.D., you will really make the most of your graduate education.

Here's what I can give you that's solid:

Campaign Fundraiser

2012 Median Pay: $50,680

Expected Job Growth: ^17%

5. RADIO, TELEVISION, AND FILM

This program is regarded as an almost shadowy, untouchable one at UT. Many kids dream about working in entertainment, but it's a highly competitive field. Hence, the limited, selective nature of the UT RTF program. If you get in, it isn't by accident. In fact, the students I've had who have gotten into RTF have been dedicated to their craft even before starting college, whether by picking up a home video camera and making amateur documentaries or by writing screenplays for passion.

One awesome aspect of studying RTF at the University of Texas is that Austin has become such a cultural hub. It's quite likely that you'll get to work on SXSW Film Festival, and you may get to participate in many independent and major motion film projects because of Austin's growing desirability.

I can't offer you any salary data because there are wildly rich and absurdly poor people working in radio, TV, and film. No matter how great you are, this is a risky field, and you have to love it enough to suffer through tough economic times

4

The School of Social Work

The School of Social Work only has one major: Social Work. Students come into The School of Social Work only has one major: Social Work. Students come into the school as pre-social work majors, and after they do their general education requirements, students then apply for the major as juniors. Social workers devote their lives to helping others, whether by working in public settings and aiding children in need of adoption or by assisting people in the hospital in accessing helpful services. There are many services and agencies available for free in our country, but people simply don't know about them; social workers help spread the word.

Some social workers opt to pursue a master's degree because that allows them to see patients on a counseling basis, helping individuals cope with their personal problems. In that field, social workers may gain higher pay and prestige and have more job options. Regardless of what field you choose in social work, one thing is certain: you need a strong sense of compassion. People often come to social workers in a state of desperation; they need a sympathetic ear and well-considered direction.

As far as résumé building to show your real interest in the School of Social Work at UT, I recommend you start taking your volunteer work seriously, aiming for some serious leadership within your current organizations. Additionally, it would be helpful if you showed some initiative by starting a program of your own – perhaps a charitable event or activity in your neighborhood. You could help clean up a neighborhood park with some of your friends, or you could help an elderly person in your neighborhood with chores around the house. You may be thinking, "But I won't be able to get service hours; how can I prove it?" While it's great to get documented service hours, that's not the only thing that matters here – social workers need to show that they WANT to do good things for others, regardless of whether they get credit for it. And, guess what else… Fake experiences are REALLY hard to describe in essays; I've seen people try and fail countless times. The authenticity of your volunteer work and giving spirit will come through in your application through your résumé and essays.

Social Worker (Bachelor's degree only):

2012 Median Pay: $44,200

Expected Job Growth: §19% (Faster than average)

5

The College of Education

The field of education in Texas is interesting. On the one hand, people say there are layoffs; on the other hand, the population is growing so quickly that it's impossible for the educational system not to grow, as well. Education is a very broad term for an industry that has many very specific components, all of which are critical to the prosperity, and probably survival, of this country. Many people start out with an undergraduate degree in education and go on to pursue graduate pathways – whether to become principals or counselors, even therapists. Education offers a strong core of communication strategies and practices that transcend the walls of the classroom, so try to see beyond the black and white.

At the University of Texas, the options for study within the College of Education itself are wide. There are ten majors within the college, all of which fall under two broad categories: Applied Learning and Development, as well as Kinesiology and Health. Not surprisingly, some majors within the college are more competitive than others, and some are programs that you can only enter after you've proven your academic merit at UT. Additionally, if you happen to want to major in something else, such as a natural science or a fine art, the College of Education can work with you to help you gain a teacher certificate through its UTeach program. I put that out there because teaching, some would argue, puts knowledge to the best use, and when you graduate, you may want to spend some time running a classroom, giving back to the community. Actually, if you happen to have a passion for giving back, you should look into the UTeach Urban Teachers program. This is a new program that leads to a teacher certificate in English or Social Studies, which prepares teachers to work in at-risk schools, where children are "all too often denied the educational opportunities all students deserve."[14] The program is still up-and-coming, but it's exciting and forward-thinking. So, even if the College of Education alone may not ring your chimes, don't let that prevent you from looking into how you can supplement your education through that college.

When it comes to résumé building for an application to UT's College of Education, I encourage you to look into each major specifically and see where you fit. Granted, you may not be able to get directly into the Exercise Science program, but if you're really passionate about the field, then you can start early by working as an assistant to the athletic trainers at your school. You get the opportunity to describe your lifetime goals in your essay, so those can include an eventual education in the field of Exercise Science. If UT expected you to have it completely sorted out before you started college, then they wouldn't have programs that require an application after you're already a student in the College of Education. Your job is to demonstrate a passion for working with people. That said, if you can specify and drill into a specific area of interest, then I encourage you to do so. If your high school happens to offer a Future Teachers program, then by all means, get involved. You can rarely show in an education career in school, simply because it's usually your priority to be a student, not an educator. However, Future Teachers actually lets you work in the classroom as a Teacher's Aide, receiving on-the-job training and even giving the occasional lesson. Since this particular college is so varied in its offerings and somewhat complex in its pathways, I am going to describe in each major how you get from freshman year to graduation, as well as where you will probably land post-graduation. Hopefully, that will help you chart a clearer course and articulate more succinctly what your actual goals at UT (and for your future) are.

APPLIED LEARNING AND DEVELOPMENT

This segment of the College of Education offers some of the more traditional majors in the field of education:

1. Early Childhood – 6th Grade Generalist

This program prepares its majors to enter any elementary school classroom and tackle both the academic subject matter and the developmental issues associated with young children. Graduates of this program are qualified to work with ESL and non-ESL students (ESL= English as a Second Language). You could walk into any elementary school in Texas and have the knowledge and experience to hit the ground running.

Now, for the job assessment: Education has been a rocky area over the last few years in Texas, particularly for teachers who don't have specialized skills. The Texas Legislature has pulled funding – lots of it – and although some of that money has been restored, schools are still stretching every last dollar. That means larger classes and less job stability. However, the population in Texas is growing every day, and we need teachers to accommodate that growth. Basically, everyone knows that teaching is tough, but in the elementary to sixth grade arena, you will have an incredible opportunity to affect the future of our state and our world. Plus, as you know, you'll get your summers off, when you can spend time with your family and pursue other interests. However, at the end of the day, teaching is about love; it's about making a difference.

Kindergarten and Elementary School Teachers

2012 Median Pay: $53,090

Expected Job Growth: ^12% (as fast as average)

- *Please note that this is the national average.*
  It's a little lower in Texas, and every district has its own pay scale.
- *The average starting salary for a new teacher in 2012-2013 was $36,352.*[15]

2. Early Childhood – 6th Grade Bilingual Generalist

As you probably know, Texas has a tremendous population of Spanish speakers. In fact, a 2013 study shows that Laredo has the largest percentage of "residents older than the age of 5 who speak a language other than English at home" – Spanish and 92%.[16] Consequently, Texas has a growing need for teachers who can provide bilingual education, and teachers with such a specialty are in high demand, making at least $2,495 extra per year right out of the gates.[17]

At UT Austin, the Bilingual Generalist Certificate program is geared towards building educators who maintain equality of opportunity in the classroom. They want great candidates who truly want to pursue a career in bilingual education. As a result, this program may be a little more forgiving of weaker test scores, provided that a student can show Spanish fluency and a commitment to working with students. If you are interested in this pathway, you will have a full Bilingual Foundations Semester at the beginning of your third year. This is a critical sequence of courses for the future bilingual educator because you have to take them all at once in a block AND get a C or better in all of the five courses to move forward. What does this really mean? UT doesn't want people who aren't serious in this program. Bilingual education in Texas is crucial to our success as a state, and UT aims to create educators that will help bring about a more successful Texas overall. Therefore, you cannot fudge your way through this major.

Elementary Bilingual Educator:

2012 Median Pay: $53,090 + roughly $3,000 bilingual stipend

Expected Job Growth: ^12% (as fast as average)

- Please note, this was hard information to really dig up because Texas has different standards than other states, and we wanted to use national information.
- Just know that teachers are not known for their high incomes, but for the impact they make on the world.

3. All-Level Special Education

Special education is a small program at UT, and it's pretty hard to get into right out of the gates. People DO transfer into the special education program, but it's a little challenging to do so because of the long Professional Development Sequence. What's that, you say? Well, it's the in-depth academic and practical experience that leads to the special education teaching certificate. While the Generalist and Bilingual Generalist Professional Development Sequences don't start until the second semester of junior year, this one gets rolling in the second semester of sophomore year. That's an additional year of professional development, so if you want to be in special education, you need to let the department know early. Otherwise, you may be very delayed in your coursework, and you may not be able to transfer into special education at all if you hope to finish in four years.

Why does this program have such a lengthy, focused Professional Development Sequence? Well, UT wants to leave nothing to chance and hopes to give students the strongest possible foundation to make a serious difference in the lives of students with learning differences and special needs. The students in this pathway learn to work with individuals of all levels of disability, as well as to prepare lesson plans for a varied classroom and to interact with parents. If you're in this program, you will get at least 1300 hours of fieldwork experience, so you will walk into your future classroom totally ready to take charge.

Special Education Teacher:

2012 Median Pay: $55,060

Expected Job Growth: ^6% (slower than average)

4. Youth And Community Studies

Some students want to work with kids, but they don't want to work in the actual classroom. There are tons of youth programs that need such coordinators, such as the YMCA, the public parks, after-school programs, and government agencies that deal with children. The Youth and Community Studies major prepares its students for those career pathways.

What's important to note is that the program requires its students to complete a minor, as well. I personally think that if a student can do the Business Foundations minor, he or she would gain skills and knowledge that would enhance his or her job prospects after graduation. However, you can minor in whatever it is you want, and if you're passionate about psychology or a foreign language, this may be an ideal opportunity for you to add those educational sequences to your academic program at UT.

Additionally, the Youth and Community Studies major requires its students to select a professional concentration from among the following four: Early Childhood, Special Populations, Coaching, and Youth and Social Services. Each one of these would walk a student down a different career path. For example, the Youth and Social Services concentration prepares its students to work with at-risk youth, specifically in the areas of drug abuse prevention and treatment and juvenile delinquency. This path could eventually lead to a counseling certificate or Master's in Social Work, so it has an open-ended set of possibilities. On the other hand, the Early Childhood concentration would lend itself well to working in a daycare setting or in a childcare-related business. Early Childhood also includes courses in working with abused or neglected children, so there could be a possible future with Child Protective Services or nonprofits that help children cope with life challenges. With respect to Coaching, there are many private coaching positions, through organizations and businesses, that do not require teaching certificates. This may be a perfect program for someone who is passionate about sports but does not want to work in the school system. Finally, the Special Populations program could lead very easily into a government position, working with social service programs. Additionally, a graduate program in Social Work would integrate quite well with this degree and would be a good future option.

Potential jobs after completing the Youth and Community Studies major:

Social and Community Service Manager:

2012 Median Pay: $59,970

Expected Job Growth: ^21% (faster than average)

These jobs are definitely on the rise because it's more important than ever that people connect with available community programs. However, you should look into the Business Foundations Minor because you will probably have to manage your program's budget and assess the program's data on a regular basis. That minor will make you more competitive.

Substance Abuse Counselor:

2012 Median Pay: $38,520t

Expected Job Growth: ^31%

Substance abuse counseling is increasingly covered by insurance, so more jobs are becoming available. You can get a lower-level certification with just a bachelor's degree, but be prepared to go on to get a master's – probably in Social Work – if you want to move up in the field.

KINESIOLOGY AND HEALTH

Many people don't understand what kinesiology is; after all, it doesn't really sound like any specific profession. Kinesiology is an academic pathway that involves the study of the body, and it's a gateway to many careers in health and fitness. As a result, the program is somewhat competitive to get into as a freshman. You will want to demonstrate your ability to succeed, not only through test scores, good grades, and a solid résumé, but also through your course selection at school.

Recommended Courses:

Obviously, you should always strive to take a challenging set of classes, but for a future in health professions, you should probably consider adding in advanced science courses and possibly a psychology or sociology class. You can also register with your local community college as a junior or senior and take an entry-level biology course; those are usually offered throughout the summer, so you can take both lower-level bio courses and get college credit at UT for them while you're still in high school. If you do well in those courses, go ahead and send your transcripts in with your high school transcripts. In addition, you can explain that you're trying to get ahead and be prepared for the curriculum that awaits you in college by taking courses in advance. You might also consider self-studying for a science AP test, even if your school doesn't offer the class. You can take the test at another school and show your commitment to going above and beyond to reach your goals.

With respect to future job options, the sky is the limit with Kinesiology and Health. You prepare for the healthcare sector, the sports sector, the fitness sector, etc. All of these parts of the economy will continue to grow, no matter what happens in politics or on Wall Street. Why? Because the population is living longer and wants to take better care of itself. Plus, sports are an incredible diversion from stress. Even in the last days of human civilization, people would be playing and watching sports, just as they have since the dawn of recorded history. So, if you're interested in Sport Management or if you want to be an athletic trainer, those fields will probably never go away, and while employment may be limited in some respects, a degree from UT always opens doors. Now, let's look at the majors individually.

1. Athletic Training

Athletic Training is a cool field. Athletic trainers treat injuries and provide emergency care for people of all ages. Trainers generally work under the umbrella of a licensed physician, but on their own, athletic trainers have the ability to come up with rehabilitation plans and provide hands-on help to athletes.

Let's not beat around the bush; the Athletic Training major is tough. They limit enrollment to just 60 students – total! And, there are important prerequisites that you must take to qualify for the program. However, you can come into the Athletic Training program from any college at UT; all you have to do is contact the Athletic Training advisors before the school year starts in the fall. That will save you time and energy because you'll get a clear pathway.

The Athletic Training program at UT begins with what's called a "Directed Observation" program (D.O.) for one to two semesters. You have to attend an orientation before signing up for the D.O., so make sure you get in touch with the program coordinators for Athletic Training as soon as possible. In fact, you can contact the Athletic Training program before the fall semester even begins, so that you're ready to get on board immediately.

The D.O. involves two-week rotations through different sports, "spending five hours per week 'observing' the athletic trainers with that team."[18] Throughout the period, students learn basic athletic training skills and go through evaluations to test their competencies. At the same time, students should be enrolled in the prerequisites for Athletic Training, which include Introduction to Athletic Training, Applied Human Anatomy, Care & Prevention of Athletic Injuries, and Introduction to Medical & Scientific Terminology. These will be rigorous courses, and your grades will be of the utmost importance in the selection process.

After completion of those courses and a minimum of 50 D.O. hours, you can apply into the program. According to Brian Farr, the director of the Athletic Training Program at UT (2014), the program is highly competitive, but many students who meet the requirements make it into the program. Yes, the program says that you can have a minimum GPA of 2.5, but competitive applicants will have over a 3.0. You may hear about people who try to get into the program and fail, but you should ask them if they really met the requirements and worked hard in their academic courses.[19]

There is no question that this sequence of courses and requirements is more intense than that of other majors, but that's because you will leave this program ready to work.

Athletic Trainer

2012 Median Pay: $42,690

Expected Job Growth: ^19% (Faster than average)

2. Applied Movement Science

This program gives students the foundation to become physical education teachers at all levels. The program involves 127 hours of coursework, and it has a great deal of hands-on work in schools. You may want to get a teaching certificate in another subject, perhaps history or math, so that you can increase your marketability by being able to teach a core subject AND work as a coach.

Additionally, many physical education teachers work outside of school with private teams as coaches to supplement their income. Or, they work with camps in the summer to get ahead financially during their downtime. As in any other field, you may have to get creative to increase your earning power, but one thing is certain, a physical education teacher has a great opportunity to interact with kids in a less stressful environment. You can really make a difference here in a student's self-esteem.

P.E. Teacher:

2013 Median Pay: $43,362[20]

Expected Job Growth: ^12%, like other teachers

3. Exercise Science

Exercise science is a major with multiple applications, but it's not generally a terminal degree. In the course of the major, you'll study anatomy, physiology, neuromuscular control, motor development, etc. As a result, you'll be prepared to pursue further education in the health professions, such as physical or occupational therapy, medicine, physician's assistant, etc.

Before going forward with a degree in Exercise Science, you should consider which graduate program interests you because you can complete your pre-requisites at the same time. You need to visit the Health Professions website at UT to find out what your course load should entail.

The Exercise Science major does require a minor, and I just throw it out there (again) that I think you should consider doing the business minor. No matter where you go in this world, you may feel the urge to strike out on your own and start a business. Trust me, it will serve you well if you have a clue about accounting, marketing, and management.

The careers I'm mentioning here are ones that do require a graduate degree because most people who go through with an Exercise Science major will want to pursue an advanced degree.

Physical Therapist:

2012 Median Pay: $79,860

Expected Job Growth: ^36% (much faster than average)

Occupational Therapist:

2012 Median Pay: $75,400

Expected Job Growth: ^29% (much faster than average)

Podiatrist: (foot, ankle and lower leg doctor)

2012 Median Pay: $116,440

Expected Job Growth: ^23% (much faster than average)

4. Health Promotion

Community health is a rising concern all over the United States. Therefore, people who are qualified to work in disease prevention and personal health improvement will have positive job prospects.

The Health Promotion major intends to encourage positive health initiatives. As such, the major includes a broad curriculum, giving students the foundation to create programs, understand health issues, and relate to others. In addition, Health Promotion majors must declare a kinesiology specialization in order to meet their graduation requirements. There are ten different specializations, ranging from Health Fitness Instruction to Medical Fitness and Rehabilitation. Check out the program's website to read the specifics.

Health Promotion majors have the opportunity to go straight into the field, working as Health Education Specialists or in government agencies. However, Health Promotion majors may also go on to pursue careers in the healthcare industry, such as medicine, nursing, public health or pharmacy.

As I have said, there are many potential fields for Health Promotion majors if they go on to pursue professional degrees, and your options after graduation depend upon what you select as your specialization in the program. Therefore, I'm just going to give you one idea of what's available immediately after finishing your bachelor's.

Health Educator

2012 Median Pay: $41,830

Expected Job Growth: ^21% (Faster than average)

5. Physical Culture And Sports

I'll come clean: I've never actually sat all the way through a football game or a baseball game. However, I'm in the minority! So many people are passionate about sports, and the sports industry generates countless billions of dollars per year. Even in recessions, sports entertainment booms because people can always appreciate the diversion. If you're in love with sports, there will probably always be jobs in the industry.

Physical Culture and Sports at UT prepares students to look into all kinds of sports-related fields, from psychology to journalism to education. As part of the program here, you choose either a minor or a kinesiology specialization. That's where you'll get to differentiate your course of study.

While many graduates in Physical Culture and Sports may find jobs right out of school, it makes sense to me that you would look into a certification program to add to your credentials and boost your earning potential. You might get a teacher certification, or you might go back for a Master's in Psychology to become a sports psychologist. If you go on the website for Physical Culture and Sports, the department has listed a host of possibilities; essentially, the degree sets you up to be a professional within the industry of sports – just not a professional sports player!

I would be overstepping the limits of my knowledge if I put potential salaries here, because the career possibilities are infinite. There's no way for me to really narrow it down. What I can say is that you may make more in Sports Marketing than you will in Sports Psychology, and more in Sports Psychology than in Sports Education. You need to zero in on your academic strengths and natural talents to figure out how you can best incorporate your love of sports into a lifetime career.

6. Sport Management

Okay, so I'm not into sports, but TONS of people are – that's why this degree is so incredibly competitive and awesome. The Sport Management major at UT provides preparation for careers in the sports industry, such as marketing, administration, and sports business, to name a few. It also might create an interesting platform to eventually go back to law school and become an attorney who represents athletes in their contract negotiations, or something along those lines.

If you want to study Sport Management at UT, you will have to apply into the program after you've enrolled at UT. Your GPA will seriously matter when you apply into the program, so even though the application materials state a minimum GPA of 2.5, shoot for 3.0 or above. You never want to be the guy at the bottom of the ladder. Put all of your effort into your first semester coursework, so that your options remain open.

This degree plan is one that spits out job-ready graduates. The school helps secure your eligibility in the workforce by requiring you to have at least one semester-long internship in a sports-related organization. The program also adds to your depth of knowledge by mandating that each student complete a minor. If I were in your shoes, I would once again make that something in business or communication, just to give you another dimension of skill in the workplace.

With respect to jobs in Sport Management, you are yet again faced with a huge array – from manager of a farm league baseball team to the coordinator of a D1 athletic department. Your opportunities after graduation will depend upon your internships during college and your grit. People in an industry as competitive as sports have to work long hours for love. Those are the people who get ahead, and there is no ceiling on their potential salaries.

6

THE JACKSON SCHOOL OF GEOSCIENCES

The Jackson School of Geosciences at the University of Texas at Austin has committed itself since 2007 to growing its program, adding distinguished faculty and building its scientific prowess. The Jackson School is home to various research centers, working on everything from Geodynamics to Sustainable Water Resources to Non-vertebrate Paleontology. Basically, this school is about more than rocks. It's developing a group of graduates who can help guide the future of our planet by applying the lessons of the past and present.

At one time, people considered Geosciences an easier back door into UT, but that is most certainly not the case anymore – if it ever was. As the petroleum industry hurtles forward, people's ears have begun to perk up every time the prefix 'geo' is used in relation to education. The Jackson School takes the best of the best.

I also think it's interesting to mention that the Jackson School offers a great deal of field experience. If you have a hard time sitting in a classroom all the time, learning only through lectures, then the Jackson School can give you a cool, new dimension to enhance your academics. Each year, the Jackson School offers programs that take students out to see the application of what they're learning. You can get your first taste of those programs even before your freshman year starts by signing up for the NeoGeo Trip. NeoGeo is for students who've been accepted to the Jackson School. Participants go to Enchanted Rock State Park for an overnight, team-building introduction to their academic pathway. Just the fact that the Jackson School offers this specific orientation retreat demonstrates the level of unity students enjoy within the college.

Now, let's talk about how you could improve your application to the Jackson School. When it comes to résumé building for the Jackson School, it would be great if you could get involved in a geoscience summer program through a local college. It also wouldn't hurt if you showed an interest in rocks or paleontology on the more basic, hobby-oriented level. Remember, you can't test out every single career pathway, and UT certainly does not expect you to spend zillions of dollars on expensive summer programs. Sure, if you can afford them, do them, but otherwise, you can start reading about the career possibilities and maybe even interview some people working in the various industries. Additionally, if you're curious about environmental systems or sustainability, perhaps you should get involved in clubs or nonprofits that focus on environmental protection. The Sierra Club is always looking for volunteers, and I'm sure that your school's recycling program could use a helping hand. If you're interested in geology itself, you could possibly contact your city's museum and see if they need volunteers of some sort in the fossils section.

You could also take some supporting courses in school, such as geology, if your school offers it, and environmental science. Additionally, you should also pursue a heavy physical science course load because a degree in the geological sciences requires a study of chemistry and physics, along with the expected slew of geology courses. Your high school course load will prove to the admissions committee your ability to manage such a rigorous curriculum. One other suggestion – if your school doesn't offer a formal geology class – might be able to take an entry-level geology course at your local community college. You may still want to take that class for credit at UT, depending upon how prepared you feel, but it would be helpful for you to know what you're talking about when you describe an interest in geological science. You'll not only sound more convincing but also show yourself as more driven.

When it comes to degrees offered by the Jackson School, the programs seem to multiply each year. Within the B.S. in Geological Sciences program alone, there are five separate options. Each one of those options offers its own valuable academic foundation, leading to a unique field within the arena of geology. With that in mind, I am going to discuss each of those pathways individually.

ENVIRONMENTAL SCIENCE (B.S.)

The Environmental Science program (EVS) at UT Austin offers an interdisciplinary approach to this increasingly important and popular degree. Students in the EVS program take courses through the College of Natural Sciences, the Jackson School of Geosciences, and the College of Liberal Arts. In fact, I have only discussed the major here, but it is mentioned in each and every one of those other schools, as well.

EVS students immediately go out into the field during the first two years of their instruction, seeing the environmental systems they are studying and gaining a firsthand appreciation of the challenges our environment faces. EVS students take core sciences in physical and biological sciences, as well as supportive classes in politics, economics, and ecology. Then, during the final two years of the program, students choose their concentration – Geological, Biological, or Geographical Science – and complete a capstone research project. Basically, when you finish with this program, you are ready to work in the real world. That doesn't mean that I think you should necessarily stop there, but you may want to get a job and see what might interest you for graduate work.

My friend, Amanda, studied Environmental Science in college, and she went on to become an attorney. She now specializes in environmental litigation and has a job she loves. The environmental science background gave her an edge to understand the environmental legal codes and inspired her with a passion to stand up for environmental rights.

Because of its concentrated, hands-on instruction, the EVS program is limited to only 50 students per year. Essentially, it's highly competitive, so if you're not a solid math and science student, you probably should stay away. Considering that the program has a calculus readiness requirement, it's pretty critical that you take a calculus course in college. I would recommend that you take Environmental Science AP and any other AP science and math courses your high school offers. Remember, if your school doesn't offer the AP test, you can also self-study for the test and take it on your own. That would show some serious commitment, so I encourage it wholeheartedly.

GEOLOGICAL SCIENCES (B.S.) Option I: General Geology

General Geology requires a set of interdisciplinary courses, requiring courses in chemistry, biology, math, and physics. As its name indicates, this is the most general of the Geological Sciences options. Most of the people who study General Geology wind up going to graduate school or becoming professional geologists. You could work anywhere from a government agency to an energy company, and your pay would definitely differ according to where you wound up.

Geoscientist:

2012 Median Pay: $90,890

Job Outlook: ^16% (Faster than average)

GEOLOGICAL SCIENCES (B.S.) Option II: Geophysics

This option requires extra course work in math and physics and eliminates some biological sciences. One of the most common industries for Geophysicists is in seismic imaging – looking into the earth's crust to figure out where oil is. You can imagine how lucrative a career in geophysics might be if you excelled in your job, given how precious oil is in our society.

I have known several geophysicists, and some have worked with software, reading the outputs of different data to find oil reserves. One friend, Steven, became wildly successful by starting his own geophysical consulting firm. He was a good entrepreneur and had the scientific foundation to back up his work; consequently, he's made millions by mapping out potential oil wells.

Geophysicist

Median Pay 2014: $94,000[21]

Job Outlook: ^16% (Faster than average)

GEOLOGICAL SCIENCES (B.S.) Option III: Hydrogeology

Hydro means water in Greek, so this field of geology specializes in solving water-related issues in our society. Whether you've thought about it or not, water is an increasingly precious resource on our planet. In twenty years, it may be even more precious than oil. As a matter of fact, around the world, people have started to refer to water as "blue gold" because water is going to have so much value in the not-so-distant future.

I have a friend, Kristin, who works for a petroleum company in the Water Procurement Division. Yes, you heard me correctly; petroleum companies are purchasing large bodies of water around the globe and buying up water rights. What does that mean to me? Well, from my perspective, it looks like a hydrogeologist may have a sparkling career outlook.

I expect the numbers below to rise as water becomes more of a pressing issue on the global scale.

Hydrogeologist:

Average pay 2014: $67,000[22]

Job Outlook: ^16% (Faster than average)

GEOLOGICAL SCIENCES (B.S.) Option IV: Teaching

As Texas continues to grow, so will its need for skilled teachers. Because of the expansion of the UTeach program at UT Austin, the Jackson School has created a plan that will allow students to complete their basic geological science degree while gaining the credentials to teach science at the middle or high school level. You would take the course work for geology – including the core sciences – but you would also fulfill a student teaching requirement and take some basic courses in instructional methods.

When you finish this program, you'll have the immediate option of going to work as a science teacher. You could also go work as a general geologist, so it basically just opens up more options for you. Science teachers in Texas get roughly $2,400 extra per year, so that's a nice benefit, as well.

Science Teacher:

Average Salary: $51,539[23]

Job Outlook: Not sure… but it's probably increasing

GEOSYSTEMS ENGINEERING AND HYDROGEOLOGY (B.S.)

This is a super cool degree program that brings together the Jackson School of Geosciences and the Cockrell School of Engineering. Students in this program spend their first two years in the Jackson School and their second two years in the Department of Petroleum and Geosystems Engineering.

All I can say is that your options will be wide open after completing this program. Petroleum engineers are in high demand, so you will probably have job offers well before you graduate.

Geosystems Engineer:

Starting Salary 2013: $93,500[24]

Job Outlook: Only looking up…

GEOLOGICAL SCIENCES (B.A.)

At UT, it can be hard to double-major, so the Jackson School created this Bachelor of Arts in Geological Sciences. With this degree, you can have a practical foundation to get a job in the real world, but you can also develop your passions in another area. I would encourage you to look into something writing-intensive or communications-related, simply because you'll open interesting doors within the geological field.

You might eventually go to law school and practice Oil and Gas Law because you'll have the academic foundation to move forward in that field. As you see those rigs pumping oil throughout the Texas countryside, be aware that there is always a legal component to getting started. Who better to hire than an oil and gas attorney? And, oil companies can afford to pay high dollar amounts per hour – not to mention that oil and gas companies very often like to hire engineers with law degrees within their own corporate environments. Play your cards right, and you could wind up a CEO. In any event, you can prosper right alongside the oil industry.

It's impossible to estimate how much energy attorneys make per year because there's so much variation. However, imagine that they charge anywhere from $450 to $1,000 per hour. Do the math.

7

THE COLLEGE OF FINE ARTS

Fine arts encompasses music, visual arts, dance, theatre, and art history. This is a niche school for an extremely motivated set of students, who find artistic and performance expression critical to their survival and personal happiness. That said, it's a tough racket once you graduate, in most cases. Many students decide to get teaching certificates at the same time that they're pursuing a fine arts degree, simply because the teaching certificate provides a clear path to a job. You've heard the phrase "starving artist," right? Well, the phrase is founded in truth, but that doesn't negate the value of the study of fine arts; it just means you need to be aware of the career struggles that may come your way, and you have to make advance plans to make sure you have a future that includes an income (ideally with a retirement plan and health benefits!).

When I look at the people who went to college with me and majored in Theatre, Dance, or Music, all of them are employed – but few of them are working solely in the performance industry. A couple have become high school drama teachers; one performs with various operas around the country; a couple of others work at restaurants and snag occasional awesome roles in plays, commercials, or films. Another one wound up becoming an attorney who represents a large makeup firm, and still one more is currently attending medical school. What does this say to you? Well, it says that the future of a Fine Arts major is far from definite. This may actually make the degree more attractive to you, especially if you're looking to expand your personality and are willing to keep your options open after college.

Now, let's talk about résumé building for this particular college. Well, these are all performance-driven majors, and it's your responsibility during high school to demonstrate talent and commitment in the area of your chosen art. If you apply for theater, you need to have all of your performances, theater courses, theater programs, etc. If you're applying for music, you need to describe your musical accomplishments – leadership roles, All-State, important recitals… If you're applying for dance, it's every dance performance, every step of choreography you've created, every important instructor who's shaped your craft. If you apply for art, you have to show a commitment to art. Put private art lessons, art shows, personal art projects, and recitals, along with anything else relevant. Remember that there's no way for UT to know you've done something if you don't put it on your résumé.

You should also take as many classes in school that pertain to your particular art as possible. Be part of the orchestra or join the Theater Club. For Dance, you may need to work with a local company, but do what you can to participate in your school's activities.

Now, I would like to break down what each separate application requires within the College of Fine Arts because you probably will have some additional work to do!

BUTLER SCHOOL OF MUSIC

Music, Music Studies (Choral Emphasis), Music Studies (Instrumental Emphasis), Voice Performance, Piano Performance, Orchestral Instrument Performance, Harp Performance, Organ or Harpsichord Performance, Jazz Performance, Jazz Composition, Music Business, Recording Technology

Applying to the Butler School of Music is a challenging process all its own. You need to check their website and make sure you understand all of the components; they could easily change after the publication of this book. Currently, the school requires a separate application. It also requires three letters of recommendation, and in some cases, it requires that you send in a tape of your music or a portfolio of your original compositions. Then, you will have to give a formal audition.

I would like to discuss the Music Business and Recording Technology programs because those sound so attractive, so romantic. However, these are tough programs to qualify for. You still have to have musical talent, and it has to be classical talent. You will have to audition for the music school, AND you will have to write two additional essays. This is not to scare you off; it's just to let you know that these aren't blow-off majors. They're also not for mere music lovers. They're for musicians.

DEPARTMENT OF ART AND ART HISTORY

Art History, Studio Art (BA or BFA), Design (BFA only), Visual Art Studies (BFA Only)

Applying to Art and Art History at UT requires the completion of a special essay, Essay D (explained in greater detail in the Essays chapter). For every major besides Art History, you will have to submit a portfolio. I encourage you to check out the portfolio requirements because they could change. Currently, they require several observational drawings and evidence of your work in different media – 2D, 3D, etc.

DEPARTMENT OF THEATRE AND DANCE

Acting (BFA only), Theatre and Dance (BA), Dance (BFA), Dance + Teaching Certification (BFA), Theater Studies + Teaching Certification (BFA), Musical Theatre

When you apply to the Department of Theatre and Dance, you have to submit a separate application and an artistic résumé, which I've always called a performance résumé. On that résumé, you will list everything you've done that relates to performance. You also have the opportunity to send in any creative pieces that represent your interest in performance, such as a script or photos of costumes you've sewn or sets you've built.

You may also have to do an audition, depending upon which major you choose. Check regularly with the website for the Department of Theatre and Dance for any updates, and get your application in early, so that you can schedule your audition in advance.

8

THE COLLEGE OF ARCHITECTURE

The UT School of Architecture (UTSOA) is one of the most competitive colleges on the UT campus. They get over 1,000 applicants each year for only 95 spots. That's a 9.5% acceptance rate, and what it means is that the school has far more qualified applicants than it can accept. However, for some people, there is nothing more fascinating than participating in the concept, design, and construction of a building or other structure.

Architects have a very complicated job. They work on more than the plans for a building's exterior; they're also responsible for working on the nuts and bolts of construction. Architects understand the placement of plumbing and electrical systems, the installation of HVAC systems, and the logistics of transportation. Architects must be well-informed about current laws and codes, and it's ultimately their responsibility to oversee the construction of their project.

Within the UTSOA lies a major that many of my students mention: Interior Design. For those students who are determined to accessorize rooms and homes, interior design may sound extremely appealing. Just keep in mind that Interior Design will adhere to the same rigorous admissions standards that every other degree within UTSOA follows.

With respect to résumé building for UTSOA, your best bet is to show your artistic and technical skills. I would encourage you to take art classes at your school and even to go through an engineering CTE program if your school offers one. A great deal of architecture and design utilizes computer programs, so whatever you can do to learn the basics of those programs would be helpful. On your résumé, you should also list any art competitions you've won, and if you can possibly get an internship with an architecture firm, that would be interesting for you to include on your résumé, as well.

In school, you definitely want to take as many classes in the hard sciences as you can. Architecture is largely dependent upon physics, so take through AP Physics C, if you can, and take through AP Calculus BC.

It's important to note that the UTSOA does not accept portfolios from applicants, so you must demonstrate your competency and passion through your résumé, course work, and essays.

INTERIOR DESIGN:

Interior Design may sound like a fun, easy course of study, but that's because there is a common confusion between interior design and decorating. An interior designer is an architect of interior spaces. Consequently, the interior design program at UTSOA involves courses in architecture, drawing, physics, etc. It's not about picking fabrics or accessorizing with fluffy pillows; it's about designing spaces that create specific moods and encourage specific behaviors. For example, a hotel may be designed to seem warm and inviting, while a hospital would look sterile and trustworthy. An interior designer is responsible for making the choices that build that atmosphere.

Since the job of an interior designer affects so much of human life, the degree is not conferred lightly at UT. It's tough to get into, and it's tough to finish. However, at the end, you will have a degree that you can use in a zillion different capacities. Yes, you might eventually want to assemble the perfect combination of animal prints, solids, and stripes in a comfortable living room, but that will only be part of your skill set.

Median Pay 2012: $47,500

Expected Job Growth: ^13%

ARCHITECTURAL STUDIES:

Architectural Studies is a four-year, pre-professional sequence. When you finish this program, you will NOT be able to get licensed as an architect. You will have to complement your studies with something else. For example, at UT, they offer a Bachelor of Science in Architectural Studies that has an architectural history focus. After you finish that degree, you might go on to get your Master's in Architecture and then sit for your licensing exam.

An acquaintance, Andrew, finished his architectural studies degree at UT and then went to Texas A&M for his Master's in Architecture. When I met Andrew, he was studying for his licensing exams (which are apparently brutal, but doable). He was working at an architecture firm in Houston when I met him, and now that he's passed his licensing exams, he's been hired by one of the top oil companies in the world. That means that you can't really predict where you'll go with this degree, but you will have to put in long hours and exert every last drop of energy to show your tenacity and talent.

BACHELOR OF ARCHITECTURE:

This is a five-year professional degree. Although it takes a year longer than your average bachelor's degree, you leave with the education you need to take the Architecture Registration Examination, which you will need to pass in order to make serious career strides as an architect.

I had a friend, Karla, who participated in a similar program, and she had some phenomenal opportunities during college. She lived in Italy for a year, studying Renaissance and Classical architecture; then, she spent an entire summer restoring frescoes in Florence. Finally, after passing her ARE, she enrolled with the Peace Corps and used her architecture degree to plan large public works projects in the Philippines. A degree in architecture gave her a rare ability to contribute to the improvement of human life, and when she returned, she could choose among private firms and government entities. Unfortunately, she opted to settle in a part of the country that has seen a decline in construction, and she's been working in a restaurant to make ends meet. That's a tough reality with architecture: You need to be where the action is in most cases, if you want predictable work and a positive growth outlook.

I am not going to list the salaries of architects here because I literally know some who make under $40,000 per year and some who make over $1 million.

BACHELOR OF ARCHITECTURE + ARCHITECTURAL ENGINEERING:

I discussed some of the basics of architectural engineering in the engineering chapter. However, I did not get the chance to discuss the fact that architectural engineering is a six-year program. Don't that let that scare you off – in truth, it's a great opportunity to square away two incredibly lucrative, respectable degrees in a relatively short period of time. In truth, I don't know any architectural engineers, but I am sure it's a wonderful job.

9

THE COLLEGE OF LIBERAL ARTS

Liberal Arts is an all-encompassing term that means (in my mind) a well-rounded, writing-intensive, analysis-driven curriculum. Many colleges around the United States – like my alma mater – are simply "liberal arts colleges," and they distinguish themselves by requiring a diverse general education curriculum. By many people's estimations, a background in Liberal Arts is impractical. What are you going to do with a degree in Spanish? International studies? History? Those are the questions people ask, hoping to force you into a corner and lock you into a more "practical" degree. Well, I think those cynics mean well, but they overlook the value of degrees that harp on cultivating original thought and that emphasize the importance of critical reading skills.

I am a product of the Liberal Arts, as are my husband and both of my brothers-in-law – not to mention many of our friends. One of my brothers-in-law, John, has an interesting liberal arts pathway. He focused on International Studies, and as part of his college experience, he studied abroad in Geneva, Switzerland. He also became fluent in French (another liberal artsy arena), and after he graduated, he went to work in Paris – by day at a bank and by night at a crowded Champs-Elysees restaurant as a busboy. What's a man to do with such experience? Well, he got hired by a French fashion company, one whose name I dare not mention but whose products never go on sale and are coveted by Hollywood starlets and C.E.O.'s alike. He works in their corporate offices and lives in New York City. John loves his life, and he would probably have had a far less colorful set of experiences if he had not pursued a degree in liberal arts.

Then, there's myself. I studied Classics, which is arguably the least practical of all degrees. For four years, I plunged into the study of ancient Greek and Latin, as well as ancient Mediterranean history, translating such classics as the Iliad and Oedipus Rex. At the same time, I declared a second major in Spanish. I studied abroad in Spain and took advanced Spanish linguistics classes, plus I dissected segments of Don Quixote and the poetry of Lorca and Neruda. Granted, these may appear to have no career relevance beyond the walls of a university, but I feel certain that my capacity to contribute to my students was strengthened by every course I took that made me write a challenging paper, every text I read that required me to flip through a bilingual dictionary, every tidbit of culturally diverse information that caused me to question my place in this world. No, I couldn't have named the exact career that would utilize my skills, but there was one.

Yes, I could have pursued a more identifiable path – in fact, I did. I applied and was accepted to dental school. While dental school didn't really cater to my natural skills (I'm pretty clumsy!), the admissions committees did not hesitate to invite a Classics/Spanish major to join their entering class. – Which brings me to another interesting tidbit… Many of the highest scores on entrance exams to medical, dental, and nursing schools are not those of science majors, but liberal arts majors.[25] That's because liberal arts teaches you how to think, not what to think. I'll never forget one Rice student I knew who was literally a genius. He studied philosophy at Rice and went on to score one point away from perfect on his MCAT. He is now a neurosurgeon, and I'll put his science know-how up against anyone's in the world.

Now, back to you. One cool aspect about studying in the College of Liberal Arts at UT is that you're not limited to just the courses in that college. You can minor in Communications or Business Foundations, or you can do what I did (and what many other students do) and take science classes in conjunction with your liberal arts degree. You can apply to a health professions school with any undergraduate degree in the world. Why not make it something you love? Something you'll never be able to study again. I personally believe that a college education is a gift from God. I hope yours will make your mind reel and your imagination soar.

Within the College of Liberal Arts, we are dealing with a vast array of degrees, more than I can describe in this book. What I'm going to do is categorize the various degrees and assess groups of majors, rather than individual majors. If you want to delve more deeply into the individual degrees and what the programs entail, you can certainly go onto the UT website and read the degree plans. However, for our purposes, it's more important to give you an overview and spark your personal interests.

Please don't take offense if my categories seem a little off! I did my best, and most of these majors fit into multiple categories.

CATEGORY 1: ANCIENT STUDIES

Ancient History and Classical Civilization, Latin, Classical Archaeology, and Classics

Based on my own college studies, I feel a strong affinity for these degrees. To me, there is no more intriguing set of stories than those embodied in Greek mythology, and there is no feeling more rewarding than deciphering the layers of meaning in a text that's thousands of years old. But, that's just me! Studying the ancient world will, in most cases, lead to a future in academia – whether as a professor or high school teacher. For students of archaeology, the path is slightly more practical, if you consider digging through desert sand with a toothbrush practical (which I do). However, it's a rocky road, that's for sure, and you have to be passionate about the field. In most cases, you will need an advanced degree to get a job – usually a Ph.D., which means probably six more years of school.

When it comes to résumé building to apply into an ancient major, you should probably take a Latin class in high school. In the alternative, you can self-study Latin. It's not too hard, and you can put your self-study on your résumé. I would also encourage you to investigate an archaeological summer program or contact a local university to see if you can assist a professor with classifying his or her findings. Nerds always need more nerds to nerd it up– take it from me; I know firsthand. Finally, these are pathways that require intense skills of analysis and deduction. The clues of the past rarely provide a clear window into exactly how our ancestors lived. Instead, we must piece through the data and assemble a cohesive picture that makes sense. That's why strong grades in AP History and even mathematics make a difference to the future student of ancient studies. Plus, you might take an AP Art History class, if your school offers it (or take one at the community college). Art is critical to an understanding of the past, so you should show an ability to recognize and analyze art and its cultural significance.

CATEGORY 2: HISTORICAL STUDIES

African and African Diaspora Studies, American Studies, History, Islamic Studies, Jewish Studies, Latin American Studies, Middle Eastern Studies, Asian Studies, Asian American Studies, Mexican American Studies, Russian, East European and Eurasian Studies, Scandinavian Studies, Urban Studies, and Geography

This is such a broad category that it's a little unwieldy. I separated it from the ancient studies because the ones above almost all center on Mediterranean civilizations; those stopped and started in the past. The other studies here are ones that continue into the present, and they affect modern life.

When it comes to history, no matter which field you select, the information you process is valuable. You may prepare for a future in a variety of industries with a degree like Middle Eastern Studies or Russian Studies, etc. You may find yourself working in a multinational corporation or pursuing a law degree that has an international focus. It might even be interesting to follow up with a graduate degree in Organizational Psychology, helping a multinational corporation handle its workforce. Another possibility might be getting a job with the Foreign Service. I had a friend whose parents were in the Foreign Service, and she had lived in such places as Egypt, Guatemala, and Washington, D.C. Her parents were well-positioned after a decade with the Foreign Service to work in many different arenas, having acted as diplomats and cultural ambassadors of the United States. This career path may not appeal to you, but it gives you another idea of international work possibilities that could relate to a degree in a branch of history.

CATEGORY 3: PEOPLE STUDIES

Women's and Gender Studies, Psychology, Sociology

I've labeled these degrees "people studies" because they look at human behavior across cultures. Psychology studies human behavior on an individual level, sociology studies human behavior at the group level, and women's and gender studies examine human behavior at the gender level. Obviously, these are very simplified explanations of these pathways. I wanted them to be; you're here to get an overview of what different degrees mean. Why complicate things with details and risk losing your interest?

Many people declare an interest in psychology before starting college, simply because it sounds interesting. Who doesn't want to know what makes the human brain tick? As a result of this common appeal, the psychology major can be highly competitive at any university. In fact, when my husband, Jamil, went through admissions training with the Texas Association of College Admissions Counselors, he was warned that students who put psychology on their application were put into a more competitive pool. One reason people are willing to brave that risk is that psychology feeds into an identifiable career path: becoming a therapist. Well, guess what? You don't have to major in psychology to become a therapist. It's your graduate school course work that will give you the credentials to coach other people through their life struggles.

Kelly, a good friend of mine, finished a major in journalism and then went back for her Master's in Psychology. The graduate program was demanding, requiring 1500 hours of unpaid internship and a heavy class load, but she is now a licensed therapist. In her field, she has a strong network of colleagues who support each other and act as a community. She also gets to go home at the end of the day and know that she provided a meaningful service to her clients, many of whom she helps move past a life of crime to embrace a healthy lifestyle. Kelly's not overpaid or anything, but she has a rewarding job that allows her a comfortable life.

I mention Kelly here because her path is one you could easily follow with any degree in "people studies." You'll have clearer direction than she did, though, because you'll already be dealing with professors who understand your career options.

In addition to the recognizable Psychology major, you might want to investigate Sociology, which I actually found more interesting in college. Sociology would set you up to follow a similar career path as psychology, but it would give you a stronger background in studying groups. As a result, you might wind up working as a psychologist in an organizational setting, helping governments or businesses establish methods and structures for handling their diverse sets of employees.

Finally, I put Women's and Gender Studies in this category because it's a growing field of study that encourages greater understanding of human experience. I could easily imagine someone with a background in Women's and Gender Studies pursuing a Master's in Psychology and possibly zeroing in on a practice that would work with a narrow segment of the population.

Despite my continued discussion of grad school in Psychology or some other counseling field, do not imagine that you're limited with these degrees. My friend, Jennifer, majored in Women's Studies, and she now is a very widely appreciated music executive, whose life involves signing bands, entertaining clients, and traveling the world. Women's Studies gave her the foundation to think and appreciate the world; it opened her mind to possibilities.

Now, what about résumé building for these degrees? Many high schools now offer a psychology course of some sort, and if you can take an AP Psychology course, I would. Some schools even offer sociology, but those are few and far between. Your community service may really make a difference for these majors: Where are you spending your time outside of school that shows your interest? One of my students who was accepted to the UT Psychology program in 2013 worked as a mentor in her school district to an elementary school student. The two met once a week before school to talk about the younger girl's struggles at home. What's interesting is that my student was the first youth approved to work as a mentor, and she had to fight for the position and navigate a ton of rules and regulations. She showed her dedication to working with people through this very special, unique activity. You have to think outside the box here, getting involved in organizations that show passion. You may be able to find opportunities through your church or school, or there may be a shelter or nonprofit that can give you the chance to work with other people.

CATEGORY 4: LANGUAGES

Asian Cultures and Languages, Italian, Middle Eastern Languages and Cultures, Portuguese, Spanish, French, and German

I think this is the time to talk about one of the most successful men I know, Robert. Robert has a rare set of language skills: He speaks Spanish, Portuguese, Mandarin, and English. With that skill set, he has a niche that's hard to fill in the petroleum industry. He can negotiate large sales of equipment – tankers, rigs – between Brazil and China, Mexico and China, Mexico and Brazil. Now, Robert's a smart man, but without his language capabilities, he would have been a far less successful one. What matters is that he started off with two languages – Spanish and English – but he didn't stop there. He went forward and added other useful languages to his repertoire. If you are fortunate enough to be bilingual, you have special wrinkles in your gray matter; you can absorb language more easily! Use those wrinkles to your benefit. Become trilingual.

In college, I added a Spanish major because I was determined to gain fluency in a language that was not only linguistically beautiful, but also increasingly popular. For my major, I did more than take language classes, however. I also took courses in Spanish art and civilization, studying the history and culture that make Spanish speakers the passionate, creative people they are. Since my graduation many moons ago, the ability to speak Spanish has proven helpful in countless situations, from my business to volunteer work to travel. I wouldn't trade my Spanish studies for anything. With my personal experience in mind, I encourage you to consider adding a language major to your portfolio.

Some people wonder why they should study French, German, Italian, or Portuguese when so ew communities in the United States speak those languages. Furthermore, the world seems to be moving towards a universal acceptance of English, right? No matter how many people learn English for business, nations will always embrace their native tongues as part of their heritage. In their home countries, Italian fashion houses will continue to run their day-to-day business in Italian, and German automakers will continue to hire people who feel more comfortable expressing themselves in German than in English. An American who shows proficiency in the home language of a specific company will put himself or herself in a prime place for hiring and promotion. So, don't discount the study of language on the basis of the growth of English. That's a shortsighted approach to language.

Aside from European languages, there is currently a large push to learn Mandarin –

and why not? A great deal of business takes place between America and China, and people who speak both languages are in a unique position to excel. Now, Mandarin is tough. It's MUCH harder than any European language, so you have to prepare to work hard. You will also need to spend at least a semester in China, immersing yourself in the language and learning the cultural traditions. China is not the United States – not in any way, shape, or form. It's not better; it's not worse; it's just different.

Another set of languages on the rise the group of Middle Eastern languages. I can certainly see the value here, especially in government positions and petroleum-related industries. Let's face it: The large majority of oil is in the Middle East. However, when it comes to oil, it probably makes more sense for men to study Arabic than women. I don't mean to offend anyone – I really don't – but the reality is that many Middle Eastern businessmen won't work with women. That doesn't mean that there aren't astounding examples to the contrary, but women probably will find better opportunities within the government or in translation capacities in private firms.

Of course, we've arrived at the résumé building portion of our discussion. When it comes to language, I recommend that, if possible, you take high school courses in the language that interests you. Take them through the AP level when it's available. If your school doesn't offer the language that interests you, it's time for you to look up a community center, where you can take language classes. I had a student who took Korean at a local community center, and I know that Chinese community centers almost always offer reduced-price or free classes. If you don't happen to have a community center for the culture that intrigues you, purchase a workbook on the internet and teach yourself. You can put that self-study on your résumé. In addition, I recommend that you take some language through the highest possible level at your school, just to show your capacity for learning foreign language. You can discuss in your essay that you didn't have access to Arabic or Italian (whatever it is that interests you), but you took what you could in school and supplemented your studies with work at home.

CATEGORY 5: TRUSTY LIBERAL ARTS STANDBYS

Anthropology, Linguistics, Religious Studies, and Philosophy, English, Rhetoric and Writing

There can be no question; some degrees are classically associated with college, and I believe these four social sciences to be among those chosen few. None of these programs has a direct job application, but all of them can shape your view of the world and make you capable of tackling any future career. However, with most of these, it's quite likely that you'll need an advanced degree.

Anthropology is the study of human development. The course work deals with the evolution of human society, and the purpose of anthropology is to gain a better understanding of our own origins. With anthropology, you may want to move on to a graduate program in anthropology itself, working your way towards becoming a professor. However, I caution you that it's getting tougher and tougher to get those positions once you finish your Ph.D. Universities have allocated so much money to science and technology, since those degrees so obviously feed into the workforce, that such softer sciences as anthropology are experiencing heavy cutbacks. There will always be positions, but they will go to extremely qualified, extremely hardworking candidates, many of them from Ivy League grad schools. Don't let that word of warning dissuade you from pursuing a graduate degree in anthropology if you're fascinated by the subject; just bear the realities in mind and work hard.

If grad school isn't your thing, you can always get a teaching certificate while you're at UT, so that you'll be prepared to go out and get a job immediately as a teacher. Our friend, James, studied anthropology in college, and he now works in the field of sustainable construction. He installs rainwater collection systems for large pieces of property, and he does well. No, he never uses his anthropological knowledge in his work, but he studied something broad and flexed his brain. Therefore, he was able to tackle new information in his current career with no problem.

Another field that's related to human development is linguistics, the study of human language. Linguistics is similar to anthropology in that there aren't many direct applications of the study outside of academia. However, the graduate programs can span a broad array of disciplines. For example, with a degree in linguistics, you can go on to get an advanced degree in Speech Pathology or Speech Therapy. You might even wind up working as a translator at the United Nations or building a computer program that mimics language acquisition.

Next, we have Religious Studies, and I think it's important to note that the Religious Studies program at UT does not limit itself to Judeo-Christian studies. You would study all religions to gain a better worldview. Granted, many Religious Studies majors may go on to become ministers or priests, but this program does not create those spiritual professionals. After studying Religious Studies at UT, you could then go on to an advanced degree in Theology, or you might decide to go to law school; regardless, you probably have some additional schooling in your future to better target your skills in the job market.

The study of Philosophy at the university level is challenging and stimulating, so it is not for the faint of heart. According to the UT Philosophy Department home page, philosophy concerns itself with three basic questions:

1. What is there?
2. How do I know?
3. What should I do?[26]

Those questions simply don't fascinate me… but they may thrill you. If so, then study philosophy. I have known philosophy majors who have gone on to become incredible attorneys, phenomenal doctors, etc. They all share a love of wisdom in common, and that's why they excel in those heavily knowledge-based professions. Of course, there are many philosophy majors who go on to graduate school and wind up working as professors or writers. Philosophy forces you to write and think on a completely different level. You will walk away from a philosophy major with a very capable brain, but you will still have trouble getting a job if you don't go for some advanced schooling.

When I was in college, English was a very popular degree. Of course, I went to a liberal arts college, filled with a bunch of literary freaks. English has become less popular with my students, however, and I think it's because English seems like a throwback to high school English class. Please do not confuse the education you will receive from a passionate professor or graduate student with what you got in high school. Even if you had an excellent high school teacher, he or she probably had to follow a preset of curriculum requirements. In college, the professors are their own bosses when it comes to the classroom. They lecture on their passions. Even if you take a basic Introduction to Fiction course, your professor has every right to define "fiction" in his or her own terms, teaching interesting material. Once you get beyond those intro classes, you'll have the chance to take smaller, upper-level classes, where you'll get incredible instruction on literature you've never contemplated. If you're not a reader or you despise writing, then this isn't the degree for you, obviously. However, if those are your passions, then don't discount English.

People with English degrees go on to do all kinds of jobs in this world. They excel on the LSAT and get into great law schools, and with the proper internships, they can find employment in the corporate world. Now, you do have to anticipate an advanced degree after studying English, or a teaching certificate. However, you will never regret honing your analytical reading skills and writing abilities. You'll be well-positioned to exceed your coworkers in the future because you'll be able to learn information quickly and present yourself effectively in emails and other correspondence.

Finally, we arrive at Rhetoric and Writing. As a high school student, I don't think I had ever heard the word rhetoric, except for its small mention in the word "rhetorical." I certainly didn't understand the power of rhetoric in day-to-day life, not to mention on the larger level of influencing the general public. Rhetoric is the art of persuasive communication; it's the sum of the skills practiced by Marcus Tullius Cicero two thousand years ago and the ultimate objective of every politician today. Rhetoric is the strategic combination of words and strategy that influences the way others think.

Whether it's convincing a jury of a man's innocence or swaying a group of people to purchase a new type of shaving cream, a meaningful message has the power to change minds. There is no industry that does not benefit from rhetoric. When you can present yourself effectively and know how to help others do the same, you hold significant power in your hands.

It's also important to note that the Rhetoric department requires an internship for you to graduate. The goal is to teach you how to apply your rhetorical skills outside the classroom. Take advantage of this opportunity because it's the internship that will affect your job prospects after graduation.

CATEGORY 6: PRACTICAL LIBERAL ARTS

Economics, International Relations & Global Studies, and Government

Economics happens to have the largest enrollment of any department in the College of Liberal

Arts at UT. I think that the degree's popularity owes to its perceived connection to business. When I have a student who wants to study business at UT but doesn't think she can get in, the first thing she thinks to put as an alternative is economics. That's because economics sounds like a synonym for money, so it seems like good, practical preparation for the real world. Since so many people share that perception, the economics program at UT has grown extremely competitive. I have seen so many students put Business first and Economics second that it stresses me out beyond belief. I would like to encourage you to consider other options than that set of majors, simply because if you're not at the top of your class or don't have phenomenal scores, you're likely not to get in. Still, I owe it to you to discuss what economics is and what it prepares you to do.

Economics is the study of how markets and consumers operate, as well as how money works. A degree in economics will definitely set you up for a career in the corporate world, perhaps in finance or real estate. However, it will be your responsibility to get internships that help target your skills towards one of those career pathways. I have also known many economics majors who have gone to law school and even a few who work in politics and government. The reality is, very few people understand how the economy operates, and if you have an economics degree, you will be setting yourself up for a leadership role.

International Relations and Global Studies is another study in liberal arts that has a clear application. In this program you look into the challenges that face humans on a daily basis as a global race. You might look into climate change, terrorism, or human rights, and you will talk about how to solve those problems. The program at UT is really amazing because it takes an interdisciplinary approach, bringing in professors from a wide variety of subjects. Additionally, it requires you to major in one of the six cultural regions mentioned in Category 2 of this chapter, as well as complete a capstone research project. Furthermore, you will select one of the following four tracks to focus your studies: (1) Culture, Media & the Arts, (2) International Security, (3) Science, Technology & the Environment, (4) International Political Economy.

The degree plan offered by International Relations and Global Studies could really set you up for any number of internationally oriented careers. You could work in any business, perhaps going back to school and getting a Master's in Business Administration, or you could go to law school. You could also work in the realm of politics, helping to set foreign policy. The important thing is that you must be thinking ahead. You have to get internships. You cannot waste a moment. My brother-in-law, John, the one I mentioned in my discussion of French language, used his time wisely. He worked in Geneva and in Paris as an intern, and he parlayed that experience into a job at an international company. With a degree like International Relations, which doesn't really include job training, you need to be proactive and pave your career pathway with meaningful experiences.

Finally, we arrive at Government, which is another way of saying Political Science. Government majors are prepared for any number of careers. I like what the UT Department of Government website says: "A government major is an intellectual jack-of-all trades who is fitted for any career that demands thought, analysis, reading, writing, and speaking about complex organizational and public matters."[27] Essentially, this is a degree for people who love to ponder practically impossible situations and search for the best solution.

While you might wind up a government leader, you might also find yourself working in journalism or as a leader in academia. Your salary prospects will depend upon where you land, but you should also imagine that a graduate degree is in your future.

10

THE COLLEGE OF NURSING

Lucky you... you get a stroll down my memory lane. My grandmother, Mimi, was born in 1911, so when the Depression hit in 1930, she was right about 18 years old. Her father lost the grocery store he had established in Waco, Texas, and had begun digging ditches, probably with the Public Works Administration. They were a family of eight, living off a ditch digger's wages, sharing one chicken for dinner, and listening intently to Roosevelt's Fireside Chats. With finances tight beyond belief, my Mimi sought a way to alleviate the burden. It just so happened that the hospital right down the road was looking for nursing students. Although she had never entertained the prospect of studying nursing, my Mimi read that the program was free of charge and included full room and board. Mimi enrolled with no questions asked. Little did she know, that one decision would bring her the greatest gratification in her life.

My Mimi adored her life as a nurse. She worked tirelessly through the Great Waco Tornado of 1953, nursed my second cousin through polio, cared for my mother during Scarlet Fever and the mumps, taught my mom how to care for me as an infant, and soon, nursed my mom through breast cancer, and taught me the value of putting others first. Nursing defined my Mimi, and the profession gave her an important level of respect – especially in a time when women had barely gotten the right to vote. Her profession compensated for my grandfather's inconsistent income. They always had a roof over their heads and food on the table. Mimi even made enough money to send my mother to private school (well, almost enough – times were touch and go). Remember, women were drastically underpaid and undervalued at that time, so financial benefits have only improved since her tenure as a nurse.

In fact, nurses do so well and work such reasonable hours that many people are turning to that field instead of other healthcare career options. I've known nurses who work three days a week and make over $70,000 per year; some make over $200,000 per year! For years, few people were informed of those numbers – but not anymore. Now that the cat has been let out of the bag, the field has grown competitive and rigorous – for men and women alike.

What's even more exciting about modern nursing is that there are so many options for specialization. You can become a pediatric nurse, a cardiac nurse, a nurse anesthetist; the list goes on forever. So, now that I've piqued your interest, I'll explain to you how to get from Point A to Point B at UT.

In the past, students started at UT as pre-Nursing students, but effective Fall 2014, students will start in nursing right out of high school. That doesn't mean that you can't transfer into the program, but it's going to become more difficult to do so, simply because the professional development sequence of the program will start earlier. For some students, this complicates the situation because it's difficult to get into the nursing program right out of high school. The program is small and selective, so it's quite possible that you will NOT get in when you apply initially. That's why it makes sense for us to discuss the full array of options.

POSSIBILITY #1: ACCEPTED RIGHT OUT OF HIGH SCHOOL

For many students, this is a dream come true. They get to spend four years in Austin, studying nursing, and they wind up with a degree they can instantly apply in the real world. In this case, you would get what's called a B.S.N. (Bachelor of Science in Nursing), and you're ready to get licensed as an R.N. (Registered Nurse) as soon as you finish the program. If you decide to go on for a graduate level of study, you will have that option available to you.

POSSIBILITY #2: TRANSFER INTERNALLY INTO NURSING

An internal transfer means that you're transferring within UT Austin. The School of Nursing at UT is very specific about the requirements for internal transfer.

1. You can only enter during the fall semester
2. You must have a minimum of 24 hours, all of which must be taken on the UT Austin campus and completed by the end of Spring semester
3. You must demonstrate language proficiency
4. You must attend an internal transfer information session or complete an online information session module
5. You must take specific courses:

   a. Intro Biology I

   b. Principles of Chem I

   c. Data Analysis for Health Sciences

   * These are current as of spring 2014. You definitely want to check the UT School of Nursing page regularly because they are allowed to change their course requirements!

6. You must maintain a minimum GPA of 3.0, with a C- or better in all science courses (in reality, your scores should be substantially higher than the minimum!)

POSSIBILITY #3: GET A DEGREE IN SOMETHING ELSE FIRST

As a sucker for academics, this is the route I would probably take. UT has an incredible MSN program, which is basically a program that gets you on an accelerated track to an RN. Then, the program takes you to on to a Master's in Nursing, which means you can specialize in a particular area –

like psychiatry or anesthesia. Whether you have realized it yet or not, nurses are starting to take a greater role in everyone's healthcare. That means they're earning more money and gaining prestige. The nurses with their MSN's or their Nurse Practitioner certifications are the ones at the top of the food chain, so take a look around and figure out where you want to be. That may help you establish how you approach your degree at UT.

I think it's interesting to mention that I don't have any friends who are CRNA's (Certified Registered Nurse Anesthetists), but I have a good friend who is an anesthesiologist. She told me that if she could go back, she would become a CRNA, rather than an M.D. That's because the median pay for a CRNA is a whopping $150,000 per year, and the stress level is pretty low. Some CRNA's actually make upwards of $200,000, so keep that in mind when you're making your decisions about a nursing degree. Work hard and keep your options open.

11

THE COLLEGE OF NATURAL SCIENCE

Natural Science is the largest college at UT. I'm not sure why I was so surprised to hear that, but I think it's because people are always fixating on the other colleges. Now that I've done so much research on the school, I can see why it's so large: It's more diverse than you've probably ever imagined, with more degree plans than I thought possible. In fact, when I first started looking at the number of pathways in Natural Science, I got overwhelmed – even scared – worried that I could not possibly bring this information to you in a way that clearly presented all of the details. However, I've gulped down my fears and given it my best go. Please know that there is still SO much more out there. This is just an outline with some brief insights. You really need to go dig through the website and make phone calls to advisers to get the full picture.

Before I start discussing majors, I would like to explain why I value the hard sciences so greatly. The hard sciences force you to examine the world around you in microscopic detail; they make you consider the possibilities of the unknown and accept the idea that all we truly have to explain what we see around us on planet Earth are simply theories. Therefore, the natural sciences are humbling. At the same time, they are door-opening. You cannot go wrong with a foundational degree in chemistry, physics, astronomy, biology, etc., because you can ALWAYS find a cool postgraduate option. You can apply to medical school; you can go to graduate school; you can even go to work and get an MBA and be a very interesting candidate in the future. Furthermore, you can go to law school and pursue the MOST lucrative law path there is, Intellectual Property. You cannot become an IP attorney without a background in the hard sciences, whether it's math, engineering, or biology. You just can't do it. So, studying science keeps your future choices broad and exciting. I wholeheartedly recommend the study of natural science if it is at all in your bones and blood. You can never go wrong.

Now, it's time to talk about what's out there, and I'm just going to go through each major. When I find that it's easier to discuss a department in general, that's what I am going to do...

ASTRONOMY

Degrees: B.S. Astronomy, B.A. Astronomy, B.S. Physics/B.S. Astronomy (in four years)

68 undergraduate students (Fall 2013)

Astronomy is one of those sciences that have always eluded me. I can't really see anything through a telescope, and I'm pretty content with my two feet grounded on solid earth. However, astronomy is truly fascinating, and at UT, the program is top-notch. It's one of the top astronomy programs in the U.S., and the university maintains its own observatory – McDonald Observatory – where students have access to the finest equipment available to study the heavens.

When you finish an astronomy undergraduate degree, it's pretty likely that you'll need to do some graduate study. Even on the Bureau of Labor Statistics website, it states that most astronomers need a Ph.D. to get a job. That's not to say that there's nothing out there without a Ph.D., but your options would certainly be limited.

I don't personally know anyone who's ever majored in astronomy, but I know it's challenging. Astronomy requires solid math skills and a serious interest in physics.

Time to talk about course suggestions: If you're interested in astronomy, then I suggest you go through at least Calculus AB/AP in high school. If you can go higher, do it. I also think you should try to do Physics C, if it's an option at your school.

So, now we come to résumé building. I had a student who loved astronomy in the past, and she spent a great deal of time at the observatory at her house. She gave classes to her peers on the locations of the common constellations in the sky, and she had a telescope in her home, as well. She was applying into physics, but we included information about her interest in astronomy on the résumé. You could do the same. There are also Space Camp opportunities through NASA, and if you contact a university with an astronomy program, you should be able to find some sort of internship position. You might also start an astronomy club at your school, even if you just showed episodes from National Geographic or the History Channel.

2012 Median Pay: $106,360

Job Outlook: ^10%

CHEMISTRY

Degrees: B.S. or B.A. in Chemistry, B.S. or B.A. in Biochemistry

(570 Undergraduate Students)

I have a soft spot for chemistry of all kinds – even organic chemistry and biochemistry; it's just fascinating to me. Chemistry is the foundation of so many different industries, from petroleum to pharmaceutical to food, and with a chemistry degree, you will have a wide array of options. Many chemistry majors choose to go onto graduate school in order to zero in on specific segments of chemistry. Additionally, you may decide that you want to work in the health professions as a doctor, dentist, pharmacist, or nurse. All of those options will be open to you with a chemistry or biochemistry degree.

With respect to your high school classes, you will need to take as much chemistry as you can, going through Chemistry AP. Next, you need to go through Calculus, ideally Calculus AP. I would recommend also looking into a free online biochemistry class, if that's what thrills you, just to know what's involved in biochem. If you want to study straight Chemistry in college, then add Physics AP to your lineup, even if it's just Physics B. If you want to study Biochemistry in college, then you could substitute Biology AP for the Physics AP.

Now for the résumé building suggestions. Chemistry is a very lab-driven science, and I think you should try to get involved in a college laboratory, if you possibly can. There are also summer programs in chemistry research for high school students. For example, Texas Tech offers its 29-day Welch Summer Scholar Program, which teaches participants how to perform research and helps them start their own independent research projects. The program even includes a poster presentation, which is a big deal in the land of science. This program is highly competitive, but it's one of many. I encourage you to use Google as your research tool and start looking for "Chemistry Summer Programs for High School Students." Finally, if none of those will work for you, do some chemistry projects at home; there are THOUSANDS all over the internet. Maybe you'll be inspired to come up with an original experiment through your exploration. Remember… report all of this tinkering on your résumé. The UT admissions people want to know you're committed to chemistry, so if you're daydreaming about the periodic table, let them know!

COMPUTER SCIENCE

Degrees: B.A., B.S., or B.S.A. in Computer Science

1991 Undergraduate Students (Fall 2013)

Computer Science is the meat of the computer industry. It's the coding and the calculations behind every single app on your phone, every program on your computer, every webpage on the internet. While I don't get computer science in any way, shape, or form, I grasp its importance to our current and future way of life, and if you're going to study computer science in Texas, you might as well be at UT.

UT has one of the top Computer Science programs in the country; nothing within 1,000 miles even comes close.[28] At UT, new technologies are in all stages of development, and the department encourages its students to get involved and find their own interests at the school. The Department of Computer Science has its own new building with top-of-the-line equipment and materials.

So, how would I encourage you in high school? Well, many schools are starting to offer programming or computer science classes. If you can go through Computer Science AP, then you should. You should also take as much math as you can. In school, if there's a computer science club, join it and get seriously involved.

When it comes to résumé building, you should start programming on your own AS MUCH AS YOU CAN. Sure, it's great to take formal classes and participate in defined camps, but nothing can substitute for your personal progress. If you write your own programs, add that to your résumé. If you take free courses online, add those to your résumé. Maybe there's even space for codeacademy.com. Literally, your goal is to show that you're a coding whiz. If you're not, you're behind.

Computer Scientist

2012 Median Pay: $102,190

Job Outlook: ^15% (Faster than average)

HUMAN DEVELOPMENT AND FAMILY SCIENCES:

Degrees: B.S. Human Development and Family Sciences

Overall, this program concentrates on studying families and individuals. The foundation is strongly scientific, which means that students who come out of HDFS are well prepared to apply to health professions schools or to start a career working with people. When I look at most of these degrees, I envision a future in counseling or education to a certain degree, and I think that's because of the natural association of human growth with school and self-exploration. However, you could apply these degrees to practically any career. Within HDFS, there are the following options:

Option 1: Early Childhood

Option 2: Human Development

Option 3: Families and Personal Relationships

Option 4: Families and Society

Option 5: Human Development and Family Science Honors (Dean's Scholars) – for future researchers

Option 6: Human Development and Family Science Honors – department-specific Honors program

When it comes to résumé building for the majors in HDFS, I think I would zero in on the concentration that most interested me. For example, I might do an independent research project on children in foster care or volunteer with a local women's center. I would think long and hard about what drives you to work with families in need because, one way or another, if you go through the academic and pre-professional sequences at UT, you will find yourself dealing directly with tough issues, such as poverty, abuse, alcoholism, depression. Figure out if this is the right road for you, and be able to explain why it is.

As far as high school courses go, I can't think of much that would be of benefit besides hard sciences, since this is located within the College of Natural Sciences, and psychology or sociology courses. This program is all about understanding human development and human relationships, no matter which specialty you choose.

NUTRITIONAL SCIENCES:

B.S. Nutrition, B.S.A. Nutrition

Nutrition is a very popular course of study. I can't get any real numbers, but I would be willing to bet that quite a few people apply into nutrition, just because it's attractive. After all, you know what a nutritionist does after college. Perhaps a nutritionist will work at a school district or in a hospital – or even on a one-to-one consulting basis. One way or another, nutritionists appear to get jobs in identifiable places, so people gravitate towards those degrees.

In 2014, the Department of Nutrition will roll out a new hybrid program, a B.S.A., so let's talk about the B.S.A. in Nutrition. The B.S.A. allows students to select minors or concentrations, such as Business Foundations or Communications. The goal is to provide students with a broad educational foundation and to prepare students with a nutrition background to go to work in a variety of industries. Remember, nutrition is part of the food industry, and that's a gigantic part of the American economy. If you're passionate about nutrition but want to work in corporate America, there IS a place for you!

Here are the options available if you go for a B.S. in Nutrition:

Option 1: Dietetics

Before I started writing this, I really didn't know there was a difference between dietetics and nutrition. As it turns out, it's not that there's a real difference; it's just that dietetics is a career pathway within the general study of nutrition. Dietetics is the route for students who eventually want to work in the healthcare industry or who want to counsel others about their nutrition. Therefore, this pathway prepares you for the Registered Dietitian certification. Within the Dietetics pathway at UT, there are other options, but those won't be as critical to your early decision-making as determining whether the overall umbrella of dietetics suits your talents and interests.

Option 2: Nutritional Sciences

This program still involves the study of nutrition, but it's really for students who want to do more research or postgraduate study, not for those who want to enter the workforce directly. In this option, you could fulfill your requirements for medical school, dental school, or nursing school (among many others). I can see how the study of nutrition could be extremely beneficial in any of those future careers; after all, many of our health issues could be corrected if we improved how we lived our lives. And, as you know, a lot of people's health problems boil down to a poor diet. With a foundation in nutrition, you could treat not only the illness, but also its underlying cause. After helping many kids apply to health professions programs, I think nutrition could be a cool degree that would set you apart AND provide the science education you need.

Option 3: Nutrition and Public Health

This is a new program that's geared towards creating graduates who can go out into the community and make a difference. While dietitians and nutritional science majors also help the community, this is more about working on a governmental or nonprofit level to encourage stronger nutritional knowledge in people of all backgrounds. I'm passionate about public health because I know that so many important initiatives are born in government-level incubators. This is really a major for people who see a need for greater nutritional awareness in the world around them and want to address it. Public health professionals rarely make a ton of money, but they can have extremely rewarding lives because their energies are directed towards improving the world. You may find genuine career satisfaction by selecting this option.

Option 4: Honors in Advanced Nutritional Studies

This program is a department-specific honors sequence. It's slightly less competitive than the Dean's Scholar program, but it's still fantastic. In HANS, students get involved in research that can change human health and prevent disease; however, their focus is still primarily on nutrition, rather than on a more general science curriculum. It is a small, hands-on program – not for the faith of heart. In this program, you would get individual attention in stimulating classes; you will work side-by-side with other motivated students; you will gain the research experience and science foundation to tackle any career. If you qualify for this program, I highly encourage it. It's like being at a small school inside a giant, world-class university.

Option 5: Nutrition Honors

This is part of the Dean's Scholars program, which is a college-wide honors program. Please check out the UT College of Natural Science website to learn more, and feel free to call the nutrition department. They are extremely nice.

Option 6: International Nutrition

UT is known for looking beyond the boundaries of the United States to give its students awareness of global issues and worldwide applicability of their studies. I cannot imagine many issues that are more pressing around the world than nutrition. We in the United States are so fortunate to have food available in our grocery stores and a government that, despite our many beefs and complaints, takes care of its people in times of need. People in other countries do not have such security. In the International Nutrition program, you participate in a study abroad trip with your class. You might go to South Africa or Ghana or rural China, and your mission is to learn in a hands-on setting. I think this program sounds amazing, and it seems like an excellent launch pad for someone interested in the Peace Corps or in working for a group, like the World Health Organization.

So, now we arrive at résumé building ideas. The people I've known who have gone into nutrition have been passionate about wellness in their own lives. That's what I would want you to highlight on your résumé: that you value wellness for yourself, and you want to share your knowledge with others. You might want to work in a nutritionist's office or beef up on your biology over the summer. Nutrition is strongly related to biochemistry, so if you want to show real interest in studying nutrition, you should demonstrate a passion for figuring out how the body works. You might even start a little nutrition awareness camp for kids or give talks at a women's shelter. Even volunteering to talk about nutrition at your church would be a great sign that you're firmly committed to this path.

When it comes to high school courses, you need to go as far as you can in math and science. There is no substitute for those disciplines. I would definitely go through calculus in high school, and if I were choosing an AP science, I would go with AP Biology. I would also consider adding in Anatomy and Physiology.

TEXTILES AND APPAREL

I'm not sure if you know this, but people wear clothes. That means people design, manufacture, and sell clothes – so I hope you're not shocked to learn that there's a gigantic industry built around the fabrication of clothing. The Textile and Apparel program at UT helps touch upon some of the key aspects of this industry through its three tracks.

Option 1: Apparel Design

Fashion design at UT is creative yet practical. Students learn how to use computers in the design of clothing because business relies upon the development of replicable models. In this program, students learn about different textiles and how to use them, as well as sustainable design, but they also focus on how to make designs that can be fabricated all over the world. When you come out of the UT Apparel Design program, you are ready to hit the ground running in the apparel industry. I don't get the feeling it's as creatively exhausting as Parsons or FIT, but it may be more practical and career-oriented.

Option 2: Conservation

Textile preservation is critical to the conservation of our heritage. Textile Conservation means the restoration of ancient tapestries and rugs, as well as clothing. Conservators may go into historic homes and help put a room back to its original condition, or they might work in the maintenance of an existing facility, exercising extreme caution in the cleaning and handling of precious artifacts. You would probably work for a museum if you were a conservator. I'm not sure there are many jobs out there for conservators, but I could be wrong…

Option 3: Retail Merchandising

For many students, this is the most practical route to pursue in the realm of Textiles and Apparel (however, I believe that all are practical if you're a hard worker and follow your passions). In this program, you learn how to design a store in a way that best showcases the merchandise.

I have a friend, Dane, who represents various natural foods companies, whose products are sold at Whole Foods. Dane not only promotes those brands to Whole Foods, but he also goes into the stores and manages their physical display. For instance, he might get a freestanding space within the store, which he would arrange and accessorize to maximize sales, or he might need to make sure that his products are visible on their shelves. That's a niche part of retail merchandising – merchandising within the store itself. The organization of the broader Whole Foods store around Dane's products is also retail merchandising. Essentially, any store you walk into has been carefully constructed to promote successful sales. A retail merchandiser is often behind the scenes, negotiating the placement of every aisle, every section, every display.

If you're a very visual person, this may be an ideal path for you. If I were to do this job, everything would be a hodgepodge, and nothing would get sold! Know your strengths...

Building your résumé for Textiles and Apparel really depends on which route you want to take once you're at UT. I would definitely investigate the pathways and delve deeply into one of them. For design, I recommend taking sewing classes and working with different fabrics – basically creating a vision for your apparel. I would also learn how to use a pattern, since a large part of your job will be creating patterns. You could do a fashion show to share your designs with others, and maybe you could even look into bringing other student designers into the event. Check out "Paint It Red" in Houston for some ideas; it's a student-hosted charity fashion show that some of my students have worked on in the past. You might be inspired to start a similar initiative in your hometown. For conservation, I think I would still continue working on sewing. I might also try to get a job in a gallery or volunteer at a museum. Finally, for merchandising, I would go to work in a boutique. One of my students got to merchandise an entire store as part of her job in high school. That could be you.

BIOLOGY

Biology is an extremely popular field of study, especially among aspiring undergrads. It's the degree that most obviously correlates with a future in healthcare, and it's almost a touchy-feely science. You can look around and see biological processes at work – from watching human development and plant growth on the large scale to identifying red and white blood cells on the microscopic scale. Additionally, many students don't see biology as a heavy math major, so they opt for a bio major over a chemistry major. However, we're going to see that biology comes in many shapes and sizes.

At UT, while you CAN pursue a very general biology path, I think you'd be loony not to look at the specialties the University offers. You only have these choices because the program is so well funded and because the professors are so engaged in their research work. If you go for the B.S. in Biology, no matter what your ideal specialty, you will start with a series of introductory courses for the first year or so that you are at UT. By the end of your second year, you will choose an option and start to narrow your studies during your third and fourth years.

Your options in the UT Biology program are exciting and broad, so let's go over them briefly.

Option 1: Ecology, Evolution, and Behavior

This option includes the opportunity to study the environment and the interactions of organisms with their environment. I had a friend who took this path at another university, and he spent an entire summer living on an island in Lake Nicaragua, studying freshwater sharks. With such experiences, you gain the ability to appreciate the value of the environment and understand how life functions within it.

Option 2: Human Biology

This option is not what it seems. You do not spend your time focusing on the human body alone. Instead you look at biology within human society. Within this broad discipline, you will go on to specialize in a particular part of human biology – like genetics or humans and the environment.

Option 3 Marine and Freshwater Biology:

The marine and freshwater option is awesome because it takes students to study at the Marine Science Institute in Port Aransas, Texas. The Marine Science Institute was the first permanent marine laboratory established in Texas. It is a highly funded facility that hosts 458 undergraduate students, and it's a critical center for the preservation and redevelopment of the Gulf Coast. You will spend a summer (at a minimum) at the Marine Science Institute, working alongside researching professors and getting real field experience.

Option 4: Microbiology and Infectious Diseases

Microbiology looks at pathogens and studies the progress of disease, as well as its treatment and diagnosis. I personally loved this part of biology, and I think the real-world application of micro is pretty exciting. If you wanted, you could work at the National Institute of Health or with the World Health Organization, studying emerging and existing diseases. You could also pursue an M.D. or a Ph.D. The options are really limitless, and there would always be some new challenge on the horizon.

Option 5: Cell and Molecular Biology

Because cell and molecular bio focus on the chemical processes within the cell, this concentration requires a substantial chemistry component, including biochemistry and physical chemistry. This is a good option for someone who loves both bio and chem, but wants a heavier emphasis on biology.

Option 6: Neurobiology

Neurobiology is an interdisciplinary program between neuroscience and biology. You would take a wide array of biology courses, but you will also take computer science, biochem, and neuroscience courses.

Option 7: Plant Biology

As much as I love other areas of biology, I just shut down when it comes to the study of plants – even though I LOVE plants as parts of my life! However, some people are fascinated by plants and how they work, and they deserve to pursue that interest. UT has an entire division devoted to plant bio, and in the end you could probably work in any field from pharmaceuticals, developing new medicines, to environmental protection.

Option 8: Teaching

The world needs passionate biology teachers, and this is an excellent program to build such future educators. You get the foundation of a UT biology degree, but you also get your teacher certification at the end of the program.

Option 9: Biology Honors

I talk more about this in the honors section of the book, but it's important to note that one reason to apply into the departmental honors program for biology is the extra supervision you'll receive. Honors will give you a stronger research background, which can only help you in your future endeavors. Health professions schools and grad programs are placing increasing weight on research experience, so try to keep your grades high and get into the honors program if you can.

Option 10: Computational Biology

My friend is finishing a Ph.D. in Biostatistics right now, and her employment opportunities within the health industry are going to be limitless. That's because she's on the cutting edge of a blossoming scientific field. With a foundation in Computational Biology, you will be in a peak position to apply to any grad program, or you could go out right away and start working in the biotechnology industry.

MATHEMATICS

I'm not sure people still spout the old "Boys are better at math" shenanigans, but I can tell you that they did when I was young. That cockamamie nonsense totally affected me because I never even considered a mathematics degree. In fact, I didn't consider myself capable of tackling any math curriculum. Funny enough, now that I'm years out from college and decades out from elementary school, I realize that none of my math insecurities were founded on a lack of talent, but rather a lack of confidence. I also know that a foundation in mathematics opens doors – more than you can imagine. You literally can do anything you want with a math degree – go to law school, go to medical school, get a job in the corporate world, become a teacher, pursue a Ph.D. The world is your oyster with a math degree. So, let's talk about the options available for the study of mathematics at UT.

Option 1: Applied Mathematics

Applied mathematics takes math and literally applies it to the problems of the world. You could apply math to almost any scientific discipline, business, government, etc. You might find yourself building statistical models to represent population change, or you might work in the realm of engineering. So many things you see around you have mathematical foundations. For instance, your microwave doesn't randomly generate a level of power; someone had to compute how much power it would generate and how much energy it would use. Your government doesn't just publish statistics on its own; it has mathematical experts who filter data and help to present as accurate and useful a picture as possible. Applied math is behind it all.

Option 2: Actuarial Science

Actuaries have an interesting crossover position between the corporate world and the academic world. They take their mathematical skills and apply them to real-world situations, specifically situations that involve uncertainty and risk. Many large companies and government agencies take on projects without knowing the exact outcomes or costs of those projects, and actuaries help to plan tactics to avoid the hemorrhage of unnecessary cash. I really can't even wrap my brain around what an actuary does, but I KNOW it's valuable. I also know that many actuaries work with insurance companies and finance companies to help them with their corporate strategies. If you're a math whiz who is also interested in business, this may be the perfect field for you. It gives you a different ability to contribute in the corporate world, and your long term employment forecasts look awesome.

This is one of those degrees that prepare you for a specific career, so here are the facts:

2012 Median Pay: $93,680

Job Outlook: ^26% (much faster than average)

Option 3: Pure Mathematics

Pure math is for deep, theoretical thinkers who tackle math for math's sake. They ponder abstract concepts, many of which might be called "useless" by people who are on the outside looking in. The reality is that pure math concepts, such as number theory, are now making their way into the mainstream. I cannot imagine that someone would happen upon Pure Math as a major; that person would probably have shown some serious math aptitude before even considering it. I can definitely see a Pure Math major as a researcher in a lab somewhere, and that's a good place for a brainiac. Don't be shy if that's you! Go after it because so few of us are actually qualified to do it.

Option 4: Mathematical Sciences

Mathematical sciences encompasses mathematical disciplines, like statistics and probability, and both of the pathways within mathematical sciences are quite practical. The two tracks vary by the focus of the program; one specializes in statistics and data analysis, and the other focuses on scientific computation. You really need to investigate these fields in more detail once you're at UT, but I want you to know that they're out there.

Option 5: Teaching

You might want to take your passion for math and teach the next generation of future mathematicians. With the Teaching option, you'll have your strong background in math, but you will also have your teacher's certificate and can go out into the world and get a job. As I mentioned in the education section of the book, math and science teachers are highly sought after. You will probably get a hefty stipend for coming in as an advanced math teacher.

Option 6: Math Honors

Math honors is a departmental honors program. It will have smaller classes and offer a strong research focus.

Résumé building ideas for future math majors include taking the most challenging math courses you can get your hands on. There are also free online courses, through Coursera and other delivery platforms, that give students access to the best professors at the top universities in the world. You can learn complex mathematical concepts that aren't taught at the high school level. Additionally, I would encourage you to get some early math courses out of the way in summer school, so that you can go through the highest math courses at your high school. If you max out on your math courses early, you can usually enroll at a university or community college to take advanced classes. The more work you do in advance, the more prepared you'll be to excel in UT's rigorous program.

MEDICAL LABORATORY SCIENCE

Wow! This is an awesome program. It prepares students to work in medical labs, analyzing lab tests for possible signs of illness. With the healthcare industry growing at an incalculable rate (well, probably calculable by a math major, but that's NOT me), there's going to be work for medical laboratory professionals.

The UT program involves 100 hours of academic work at UT (minimum). Then, you go on to medical laboratory science program, such as the one at the Methodist Hospital in Houston, to get your clinical education. You will then be able to sit for your certifying exams with the American Society for Clinical Pathology. You will be fully prepared to get a job in an exploding field.

2012 Median Pay: $57,580

Job Outlook: ^22% (much faster than average)

If you want to start building a résumé for Medical Laboratory Science, then I suggest you show an interest in lab science at school and in your extracurricular activities. I would try to get an internship in a medical lab in your area. Almost every doctor sends blood tests out to a lab, so talk to your physician and see if you can contact the lab he or she uses. You might also volunteer at your local hospital, and perhaps they will let you take patients back and forth to their testing. It might not expose you to what the scientists themselves are doing, but it will make you keenly aware of the human element on the other end of the tests that you will eventually perform.

You will also want to go through the highest levels of science and math that your school offers. If you can possibly get involved with any student research projects, I highly recommend that you do so,

NEUROSCIENCE

It's incredible that UT has an entire program dedicated to the study of the brain. The undergraduate program at UT introduces its students to fundamental sciences, but it also concentrates on research, using the most advanced technologies. Undergraduate students use such techniques as MRI, live cell imaging with two-photon microscopy, and intracellular electrophysiological recording. How awesome is that? It's also wonderful that the program at UT encourages students to get involved in research from early on. You can even start as a freshman and build a body of comprehensive skills; you might even wind up being mentioned in the byline of a publication.

At the end of a degree in neuroscience, you may will probably find yourself doing research in the medical arena. However, you could work in pharmaceutical sales or apply to medical school. One way or the other, you will have career options, and you will have an intriguing four years of study to figure out which direction you want to pursue.

When it comes to résumé building for neuroscience, I encourage you to take the highest levels of math and science your school offers. I also think you could possibly volunteer at a facility that takes care of patients with Alzheimer's and/or dementia. It's good to work firsthand with the patients whose conditions you are going to study, not only because you see the symptoms and behaviors in real life, but also because you'll become acutely aware of the need that drives your study. There are also summer programs that teach high school students about neuroscience. For example, there's a Northwestern Neuroscience Camp at Northwestern College in Iowa. Google it if it interests you. If you can't afford to do such a program, contact a nearby doctor's office or a university and attempt to shadow or get an internship. In the alternative, you could come up with a cool fundraising idea that would help you pay for the trip. The Northwestern program costs $650 (2014), and if you let members of your community know your goals, they might help you raise that sum of money. You should definitely describe that you went to those lengths in an essay!

PHYSICS

The Department of Physics at UT has 270 undergraduate students and 227 graduate students. To me, that sounds small, but it's apparently one of the largest in the country. Amazingly, in that large program, almost all of the courses are taught by actual faculty, not TA's or grad students. That's probably why the school has received so many accolades for its academics.

In Physics, you start off with an introductory sequence of courses: Mechanics and Motion, Waves and Optics, and Electricity and Magnetism. You'll also be taking high-level math courses and working your way through the UT core curriculum. When you finish your intro classes, you move onto one of four options: Physics, Computational Physics, Radiation Physics, or Space Sciences.

Since you don't have to start targeting yourself towards a particular pathway until your junior year or so, I encourage you to just think about whether or not physics thrills you as a science. I find it fascinating, and a background in physics is something you will never regret having.

If you want to build your résumé for physics, you need to concentrate first on your academics. You should definitely go through Physics AP and Calculus BC. Then, you should consider working on some cool physics projects. You might google high school physics projects and begin by using a template for a project that already exists. Physics is all about pushing the boundaries of knowledge, so you could complete a previously designed project and then find a way to modify it to come up with your own investigation. You can also contact a university and see if you can sit in on some college physics course, or call a physics department and see if you can work as a lab assistant.

PUBLIC HEALTH

The population of Texas is growing by the day, and every Texan will require health services at some point in his or her life. That's why UT has created the undergraduate degree in public health – to build the public health workforce. You cannot come straight into the UT Public Health program as a freshman; instead, you have to take a series of prerequisite science courses and maintain a minimum GPA of 2.75.

If you are passionate about helping other people and if you want to work in healthcare but aren't sure which specialty suits you, the public health route could give you a good foundation to make a decision. Since the program is so new, there isn't as much information about it as there is with other degree options. However, you can always call the school itself and ask questions. I have worked with many people who had their Master's in Public Health but not so many who were working on a bachelor's. Therefore, I don't feel like I can speak with as much authority as I would like.

To build your résumé and flesh out your interest in public health, I recommend that you look for a volunteer position with an organization that promotes community health. For instance, I googled "Health and Human Services Volunteer Houston" and found several opportunities here. I suggest you do the same in your hometown. You can also volunteer in a hospital, even if it's just helping people find their way around, or you can participate in health events at your school. Whatever it is you do, try to forge your own path. Put a group of volunteers together for a fun run, or organize a blood drive. Public health is all about spreading awareness and taking charge of a situation, so show that you have the gumption to take on a new task and push a message. In school, you should try to take challenging sciences, but you would also be well-served to take a psychology or sociology class. With public health, you're always trying to affect people's behavior and improve their wellness, so it's good to know how people think and how you can best approach others.

12

THE McCOMBS SCHOOL OF BUSINESS

I'm a little less enthusiastic about a business major than many other people are. While I can see that it's a pragmatic course of study, I also like the prospect of teaching students to think outside the box. However, this book isn't my soapbox, and I must acknowledge that business majors finish college with useful skills. That alone makes it worth the investment of time and energy.

It is true that the McCombs School is extremely difficult to get into, so I wouldn't count on this as your first choice unless you're at the tip-top of your game. That means that even if you're at a highly competitive school with awesome grades (but not top 7%) and phenomenal test scores, you can get a rejection letter. It's shocking but true. If this is your passion, it's difficult to advise you on what to do. The reality is that even getting into UT through a different major and transferring into the McCombs School is a serious challenge. You would need somewhere in the range of a 3.9 GPA. Consequently, you need to think long and hard before putting Business as your first choice. If you are passionate about business, then you probably need to apply to an array of schools. You can't fixate on McCombs; it's just impractical. Put your best application together and let the chips fall, but apply to other schools, too! Even students in the top 7%, who are automatically admitted to UT, can get rejected by McCombs. It's brutal but true.

In McCombs, you will have multiple majors to choose from. While many of you may be familiar with the possible business majors, I think it's still important to give you a few details and toss in my two cents.

ACCOUNTING

Many people are simply not cut out for accounting. It's a detail-oriented field that would eat me alive, and my husband, whom I consider a genius, got his only C in accounting. That's because it's tough. And because it's tough, good accountants are highly prized in our society. Accountants prepare people's taxes and make sure that organizations are conforming to the law. As an accountant, you will always have a job – especially if you become a CPA, a Certified Public Accountant, which requires an extra exam after you complete your degree in accounting.

2012 Median Pay: $63,550

Expected Job Growth: ^13% (As fast as average)

BUSINESS HONORS, OFTEN REFERRED TO AS BHP

This is an extremely competitive honors program within the McCombs School. Only the most qualified, motivated students receive an admissions offer from BHP. The program is strictly limited in size, and it creates a community that is supportive and strong. BHP is a major on its own, but students still specialize in Finance, Accounting, Marketing, etc. Please refer to the Honors program section of the book for more details.

SCIENCE AND TECHNOLOGY MANAGEMENT

Yeah, this program is pretty amazing; it combines business and engineering into one degree plan! You will take management courses and basic business classes, but you will also get the chance to take engineering classes in a variety of disciplines to build a real understanding of what's going on with the engineers you will eventually help to manage.

There isn't any real way to sort out what the pay is for a job that would follow this degree because it's applicable to so many different career pathways. Just know that you should have an array of options.

FINANCE

Are you obsessed with the stock market? Do you think about investments, even though you have very little to invest as a high school student? If so, Finance may be the right field for you. With Finance, you can work in a variety of industries, and within the Finance major, you can choose to specialize in one particular area of business.

Financial Analyst

2012 Median Pay: $76,950

Expected Job Growth: ^16% (faster than average)

INTERNATIONAL BUSINESS

We may live in our comfortable, confined communities, but we live in a global society. We probably purchase more goods made abroad than made in the U.S., and our economy is so entangled with that of Europe, China, and the Middle East that it's almost surreal to study our isolationist policies of the past. As a consequence, International Business is a very practical, forward-thinking major. Considering the scope of international businesses and their transactions, I can't think of any way to zero in on a specific job and its prospective pay and growth. The sky is the limit.

MANAGEMENT

All organizations need leaders. That's why there's a Management major and why it's so popular. You will learn how to lead a group and how to plan for the future. With a Management background, you could really work in any industry. Maybe you'll even create something totally new. You'll have the education to make that happen after finishing a Management major at UT. That said, you will probably need to go after an MBA eventually because you'll reach a ceiling if you don't get an advanced degree. You could also make yourself a real threat by doing a joint MBA/JD program. In the end, you would have business knowhow to run an organization AND the legal authority to negotiate contracts. The career possibilities after finishing a degree in Management are endless, so to discuss salaries or prospects would be folly. Your potential is limited only by your imagination.

MANAGEMENT INFORMATION SYSTEMS

MIS is a business major that focuses on IT and computer aspects of business. You will gain the ability to lead a team, but you will also understand how businesses can and do manage the voluminous data that accompany countless transactions, numerous personnel, etc. You will also learn programming in this major, so if you have a natural inclination towards Computer Science, this might be a nice marriage of that interest and business

Information Systems Managers

2012 Median Pay: $120, 950

Expected Job Growth: ^15%

MARKETING

Marketing is all about sales; it focuses on identifying consumer tastes and figuring out how to reach out effectively to large groups of potential buyers. You might wind up doing marketing for a title company or for a large restaurant company or for a college.

What I like about marketing is the social aspect of the field. I have a good friend, Liz, who worked in marketing for multiple organizations, and she's always doing cool things, meeting cool people and attending cool events. If you're anti-social, this may not be the right major for you.

Market Research Analyst

2012 Median Pay: $60,300

Expected Job Growth: ^32% (Much faster than average)

SUPPLY CHAIN MANAGEMENT

(Sometimes Called Logistics)

Manufacturing goods is pretty worthless if you can't get the products efficiently to the consumer. Supply chain management is the field that helps facilitate the seamless acquisition, distribution, and delivery of products. As the global economy continues to expand, so will the need for educated supply chain managers.

Logistician

2012 Median Pay: $72,780

Expected Job Growth: ^22% (Much faster than average)

Now, let's talk about résumé building for an application to the McCombs School. Some schools offer great business programs, such as Academy of Finance or Business Professionals of America. If yours does, I highly recommend that you get involved. I also recommend that you get a job, and if you have access to an internship at a company that interests you, then by all means take it. You might even be able to pick up a phone and call a local business to see if they would let you work for free for a few weeks, so that you could learn a little bit about business activity. You could also start something entrepreneurial, perhaps even a charitable effort. Whatever it is, you want to show leadership and innovation. McCombs is creating the leaders of tomorrow, so show them you're already making headway in that direction.

In school, you need to go through Calculus, ideally AP Calculus AB or BC. You should also work on your other basics, especially those that are writing intensive, such as English and history because those areas show critical thinking skills. You need to concentrate on maintaining as high a GPA as possible because there are too many amazing applicants to McCombs for them to forgive even one slacking semester.

BUSINESS FOUNDATIONS CERTIFICATE

I was tempted to give this certificate its own chapter. I've mentioned it countless times throughout this book because I recommend it to students pursuing almost any academic pathway. The Business Foundations Certificate is a program that's available to any non-business student at UT, and it's a great way to add career-enhancing courses to your education. In the 24-hour sequence, you'll take such standard classes as economics, statistics, accounting and information systems. Then, you can specialize in either a General or Global Track, depending upon your interests. You should definitely go onto the website and read about your options; this certificate can only boost your chances of employment and open doors. Therefore, even if it sounds tough, it's worth the effort.

13

THE SCHOOL OF UNDERGRADUATE STUDIES

I mention the School of Undergraduate Studies throughout this book, but it really deserves its own section. I was reluctant at the outset to include it because you can't MAJOR in Undergraduate Studies. However, Undergraduate Studies is a very valuable academic option at UT because it gives students a chance to begin taking courses at the University of Texas before they formally commit to a major. As a person who flip-flopped six thousand times before landing in the right field, I can vouch for the value of entering college undecided.

Undergraduate Studies offers comprehensive advising to its students (and even to students outside UGS). It's the right choice on an application for someone who has great academic credentials and a history of leadership but has yet to settle on a major.

I wish I had more to say about the school, but I think you should really contact them on your own, since there are so many pathways when you arrive at UT. You might wind up in accounting or human ecology; it all depends on what courses you register for and what grades you make when you get here. Call UGS and ask for more details.

14

UNIVERSITY STATISTICS

While I really don't want you to dwell on numbers, I know that people can't help but have questions about statistics. So, I have plowed through the pages on website of the UT Office of Information Management and Analysis to try to put together some data that may be useful to you. Every number I have used here is freely available to ANYONE who wants to go on that site. Frankly, there's more information there than many people might ever want to consider.

If you want to go on that website and start doing some browsing, you're more than welcome to do so. What you won't find is a golden ticket to admission – beyond staying in the top 7% of your class.

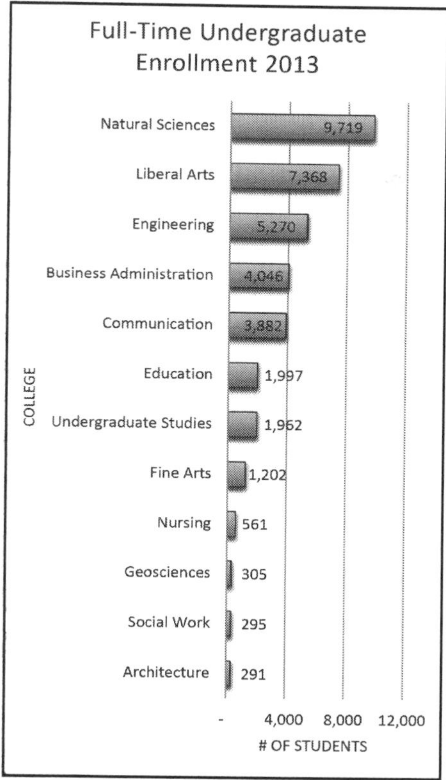

Figure 1 [29]

Figure 1 gives you a breakdown of the undergraduate enrollment in each college at UT. While these numbers may not substantially influence your life, they show you that the University of Texas is not just one giant pool of students. The different colleges have varying levels of enrollment. People are often baffled that their kids don't get the major they want at UT, and this may help you understand. There simply isn't unlimited space in each program.

Now, these numbers may be deceptive. Don't think that just because a school has a higher number of undergraduates, it's less competitive to get in. The competitiveness of UT majors fluctuates each year. All you can do is put together an application that shows your passion and talent for a particular major.

Looking at this, you can also see how a massive application shift might affect admission. For instance, if people hear that Geoscience might be an easy backdoor and start applying there in record numbers, Geoscience will max out in a heartbeat. It might even become more competitive than one of the larger majors because there's only so much space. The moral of the story: Backdoors are illusory.

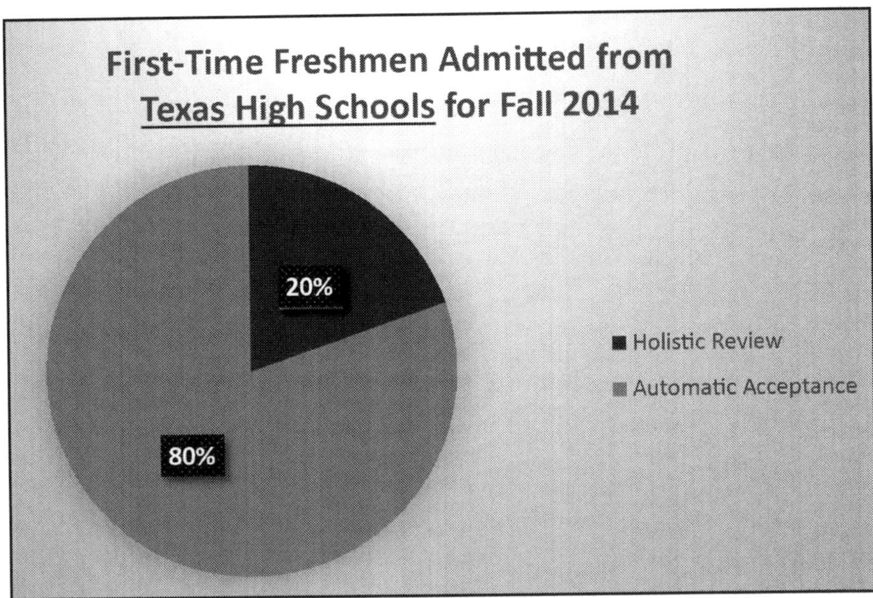

Figure 2 [30]

Sometimes, people hear about the top 7% rule, but they don't really understand how it affects the situation. Wrap your brain around *Figure 2*. This is how acceptances to UT shake out for first-time freshman applicants from Texas high schools. Since UT is a state school, it is bound to accept the large majority of its students from Texas, so although you can't take these percentages and describe the entire entering class, you can get a reasonable picture of how many automatic applicants there are to UT. This may help you come to grips with the fact that there can be tens of thousands of UT students, but not enough spaces to let in all the smart kids who apply. There is a helpful letter, which I mention in the endnotes, released by the Office of Information Management and Analysis, that gives some recent enrollment statistics. That's where I found the data for *Figure 2*, and it may be useful for you to check it out. You can find it on their website.

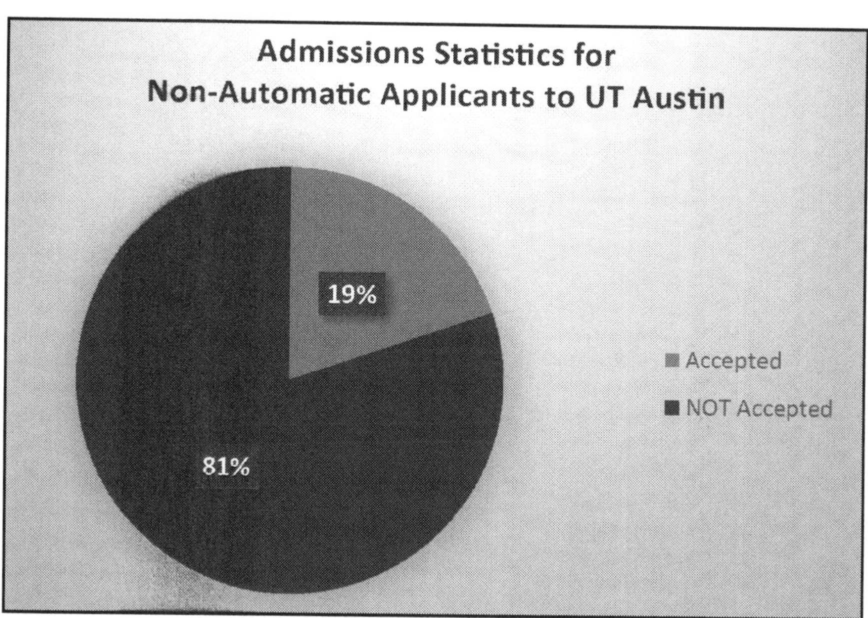

Figure 3 [31]

As part of my agreement with the University's Office of Information Management and Analysis, I can't release the actual numbers of non-automatic applicants to UT, but I can tell you that the acceptance rate was 18.9%. That percentage includes both in-state and out-of-state admitted students! I can also tell you that the overwhelming majority of applicants to UT were not automatic. I think it's important for you to know this percentage because it's lower than the published acceptance rate of 20% for the extremely competitive University of Southern California![32] The published acceptance rate for UT is 40%, but that includes both automatic and non-automatic admits.[33] I know many students look at that 40% acceptance rate and consider it Gospel, but they really should not do so. They need to see UT admission in two camps. First, if you're in the top 7%, consider it a 100% acceptance rate (although not necessarily to the major of your choice). Second, if you're not in the top 7%, consider it as challenging as any other highly competitive college.

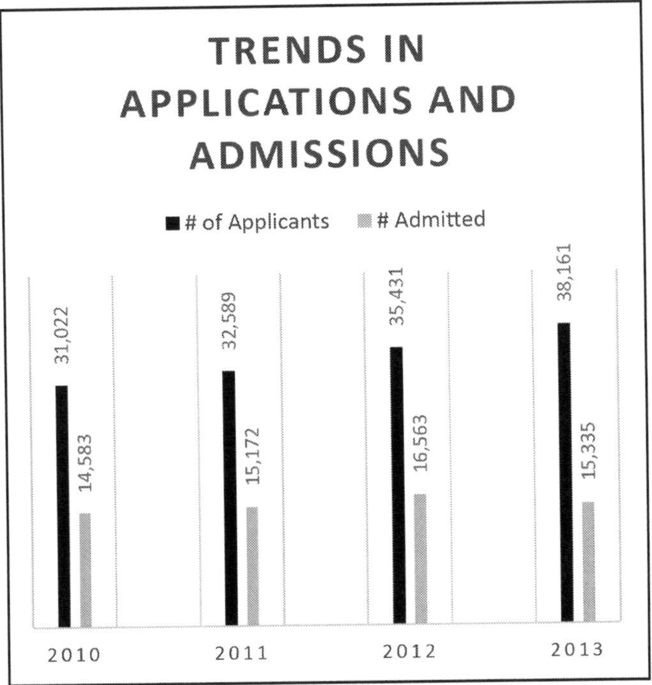

Figure 4 [34]

I included Figure 4 to show you that UT's application numbers have risen each year – an increase of over 7,000 since 2010. However, the University has limited space, so the number of admitted students has only risen by 1,000 in the same time period. I want you to see that the perceived competitiveness in the UT admissions is real. Still, you can still find a pathway to UT, no matter what.

TEST SCORES

As silly a measure as test scores may be, they're required, and they can influence acceptance. In fall 2013, the average SAT scores was 1872, so you can imagine a 600 or above in all sections on average.[35] The ACT average was 28.[36] It's important to note that automatic admits also submit test scores, and those may be lower because automatic admits don't have to stress over their final scores.

If you are NOT automatic, I think you should imagine you'll need higher numbers!

Additionally, while no one will say it and nothing is hard and fast, there is a minimum threshold for non-automatic students, and it's set by the state of Texas. The Texas Success Initiative is a state program that aims to make students more successful in college by using test scores to assess readiness. Students who fall below certain test scores are considered unprepared/ineligible to take college-level courses. For most entering freshmen, these are the requirements to take regular, non-remedial courses:

- *A student with an SAT score of at least 1070 and a math score of at least 500 is exempt from the math requirement*
- *A student with an SAT score of at least 1070 and a critical reading score of at least 500 is exempt from the reading and writing requirements*
- *A student with an ACT composite score of at least 23 and a math score of at least 19 is exempt from the math requirement*
- *A student with an ACT composite score of at least 23 and an English score of at least 19 is exempt from the reading and writing requirements*
- *A student with an exit-level TAKS math score of at least 2200 is exempt from the math requirement*
- *A student with an exit-level TAKS English/language arts score of at least 2200 and an essay score of at least 3 is exempt from the reading and writing requirements*
- *A student with a score of at least Level 2 on the STAAR English III end-of-course (EOC) is exempt from the reading and writing requirements*
- *A student with a score of at least Level 2 on the STAAR Algebra II end-of-course (EOC) is exempt from the math requirement*[37]

Students who fall below these minimum numbers are required to take remedial courses, and they are often delayed in graduation. Furthermore, they often need assistance with preparing for the Texas State Initiative exam, which is administered to students who are not exempt. This costs a university money and time, and although no one will come right out and verify my thoughts, I can't see why UT would take a non-automatic admit who wasn't exempt. They are already bound to take automatic admits, regardless of their scores, and they have committed to invest their energies in those students. Why would they add to their burden, unless an applicant was truly extraordinary in some other way? Perhaps if you're a budding Picasso or a musical prodigy, or if you've solved some age-old mathematical riddle, someone will be willing to dip below the TSI standard, but otherwise it seems unlikely.

If you DO NOT meet these TSI numbers, I really encourage you to spend some time at your local community college, squaring away your developmental courses. You could find yourself in a world of hurt at a school as competitive as UT Austin. These numbers are in place to propel Texas students towards success, not to stymie their efforts to reach their goals.

In any case, please prepare for your SAT and ACT. Don't go in blind. I don't care how smart you are; you need to take some practice tests and get comfortable with what awaits you. Low scores never work to anyone's advantage, so do your best, even if you're automatic.

15

THE APPLICATION ITSELF

As you probably know, UT's application is located on ApplyTexas, a statewide application site that goes out to almost every school in Texas. ApplyTexas has some basic components, including the application itself and the essays. However, in addition to the application, most students also send in a supplemental résumé and have extra forms to fill out on the "BeALonghorn" site after they've applied. I want to use this opportunity to talk about the résumé and the essay topics.

RÉSUMÉ

A college résumé is nothing like a job résumé. It's not a one-pager; it's a detailed record of your involvement and achievement in high school. Many students don't understand the scope of the college résumé, but I'm here to tell you that it can be upwards of 6 pages long. Your goal in the résumé is to do more than just show what you did; it's about showing why you did it and what you learned from it. Don't hesitate to add an extra line of description or another level of detail. They want it all.

On our website, we have developed what's called a Résumé Builder, which follows the suggested UT format to a tee and matches nicely with other applications' requested formats. You can check out the sample résumé on our site, and then you can decide if you want to use our Résumé Builder or just mimic the format on your own. One way or another, that's the look you're going for.

When I work privately with students, I encourage them to consider renaming the categories on their résumés after they download them. For example, where we have the "Activities" section, some students will list career-specific activities. If they want to go into education, they will put their Future Teachers activity there, as well as their Sunday school leadership or their camp counseling experience. Then, they will rename the section "Educational Leadership" or "Educational Experience." I encourage you to consider that sort of strategic grouping in your own résumé, especially if you've put a great deal of energy into a few important areas. For example, even if you don't want to study music, you might want to make "Musical Activities" its own category; after all, if you've spent hours upon hours studying, practicing, playing, and competing, you should showcase that dedication.

To get moving in that direction, I encourage you to type out or scrawl out a list of everything you've done since the summer before 9th grade. Take a look at the many activities and start to rearrange them, organizing them into categories. You may find that the standard categories fit you best, but if you see another pattern emerge, then consider whether or not you should invent an additional category.

Sometimes, students get confused about how to account for their community service involvement. What I encourage is for students to put their service organizations under Extracurricular Activities and to separate out the actual service experiences. That way, you can describe your leadership and participation in the organization in Extracurricular Activities, but you can describe your service and list your hours under the Community Service umbrella.

There is no specifically right way to create a college résumé, so use your imagination and remember that the admissions committee knows very little about you. This is a chance to show how hard you've worked to earn a place at the University of Texas at Austin.

Don't forget to upload your résumé through the UT MyStatus page! You do this AFTER your application has been submitted. Also, be sure to put your UT EID on the top of the résumé.

ESSAYS

UT Austin has five potential essay topics: A, B, C, D, and S. Every student is required to submit Essay C, and then, they must choose from Essays A, B, and D – at a bare minimum (Many students send in 3 essays). Additionally, although it is not on ApplyTexas, students have the option of submitting Essay S through their UT application portal. I'm highlighting the words I want you to evaluate individually because they're open to interpretation and should be carefully considered before you plunge into writing.

Let's start by talking about Essay C, since everyone will write it:

Essay C

Considering your **lifetime** goals, discuss how your current and future academic and **extra-curricular** activities might help you achieve your goals.

This is the **exact** topic we address throughout this book – what are your goals and how **are you** trying to get there? As I've said in so many speaking engagements **and in** intimate settings with families, for most of my students, their lifetime **goal was** to get into college. Teenagers often think of life in terms of **short-term** milestones, and with the broad curriculum they see in high school, **they don't** really get the chance to develop passion. Well, that doesn't really **make** for a compelling essay, nor does it demonstrate that a student can **excel in a** given field at a school as competitive and challenging as UT Austin. **It's time** for you to sit down and think about what you've done and how those **activities** reflect your interests.

I feel like **this is** a prime time to discuss the School of Undergraduate Studies because **if you** are undecided about what you hope to study at UT, then you should **put** Undergraduate Studies as your first choice. Then, you should use **your essay** to discuss your drive towards academic excellence and your desire to be a leader in your community – maybe to go to medical school or to become a teacher. Go on to explain that you know that you can major in almost anything to achieve those goals, and you are looking for your academic passion. You want to enter through Undergraduate Studies in order to see all of the options that are available to you at UT Austin and find your niche.

Remember not to list your achievements or retell your résumé in this essay. This essay is about describing how your achievements, academic pursuits, and activities are driving you towards your goals. Sit back and reflect on which parts of your résumé you would like to highlight in this essay and tell a story that frames the importance of those experiences in your life.

Essay A

Describe a setting in which you have collaborated or interacted with people whose experiences and/or beliefs differ from yours. Address your initial feelings and how those feelings were or were not changed by this experience.

Ugh, this topic is just NOT my favorite, but I can't do anything about it. We have to discuss it!

When considering this topic, I encourage you to look at each word individually and try to imagine different scenarios in your life that might fit the bill.

"Collaborate" could mean working on a project in school together, or it could mean planning an event. It could also have something to do with a summer program or an organization to which you belong. You're trying to think of times when you didn't act alone, when you had to consider others' opinions and feelings.

"Interact" is a broader term than collaborate, and it leaves a little more wiggle room. Have you volunteered in a community that was unfamiliar to you? Have you taken a class with people you didn't know or gotten a job and met a whole new group of people at once? Well, one of those situations may apply here.

The tough part is that there's a qualification: The group has to have beliefs or experiences that differ from your own. That means you really need to step outside your comfort zone and attempt to define those words in the context of your own life experience. For example, you might have religious beliefs that are different, or you might have ideas on how to plan a project that are different. Any experience is worth considering and exploring in greater detail.

Your goal is to show how you've grown as a result of these experiences. You might walk away firmer in your beliefs or more confident in yourself, or you might develop a greater understanding of someone else's background. Furthermore, you might develop a better understanding of how to come to a compromise or how to accept someone else's right to personal opinion without sacrificing your own.

Essay B

Describe a circumstance, obstacle or conflict in your life, and the skills and resources you used to resolve it. Did it change you? If so, how?

This is a pretty standard topic. It's an opportunity to discuss parts of your life that haven't been perfect, and it's a chance to discuss the effects of those experiences on your character. I want you to understand something here – you don't get anywhere in the realm of admissions by lying or hiding experiences. You have to come clean with the admissions committee, especially if there's a discrepancy on your transcript for some reason. I once had a student whose grades suffered tremendously because she broke her back in 10th grade. She was in the 3rd quarter of her class, but she still got into UT. Why? Because she gave a solid explanation of the circumstances and the negative effects her condition had on her grades. She was able to show that her grades before and after that incident had been solid. The admissions committee saw that she had faced and overcome a serious obstacle, and she was able to prove that she had the tenacity and intellect to succeed at UT. This essay gave her the platform to provide that explanation.

Sometimes, the obstacles in your life might not be as obvious, or they could be even more embarrassing and personal. I encourage you to dig deep and think about what aspects of your life have not been storybook perfect – perhaps there are a lot of them, and perhaps not. I haven't met many kids whose lives had been totally free of struggle.

Now, speaking as an advisor to you, I have to warn you that while I want you to come clean, I want you to also take into consideration the impression your essay will give about you as a student. I know that so many people suffer from eating disorders, for example, and such self-esteem issues take a serious toll. However, I always worry that when an admissions committee reads an essay about a lingering psychological issue, like an eating disorder, they can't help but wonder how you'll handle the pressures of college. No one wants you to come to college and suffer from severe depression or starve yourself. It's not that I don't think you should tell your story, but make sure you explain how you have handled and RESOLVED the issue. You want the admissions committee to feel confident that you can survive in the high-pressure environment of the University of Texas.

In any case, you should definitely take advantage of this essay if you have been through any challenging situations at all. It's a classic essay topic that gives you ample leeway to describe any hurdles you've surmounted in your life so far.

Essay D

Submit this essay (along with Essay C) if you are applying to architecture, art history, design, studio art, or visual art studies/art education.

Personal interaction with objects, images and spaces can be so powerful as to change the way one thinks about particular issues or topics. For your intended area of study (architecture, art history, design, studio art, visual art studies/art education), describe an experience where instruction in that area or your personal interaction with an object, image or space effected this type of change in your thinking. What did you do to act upon your new thinking and what have you done to prepare yourself for further study in this area?

Since this essay is major-specific, only a few of my students wind up writing it. However, what I have seen be successful is an approach that describes a particular form of art or a specific piece of art (even if it's a space of some kind). You should choose something that's related to your chosen major. If you are interested in architecture, describe a space or building or sculpture – something that inspires you to create and study architecture. If you are passionate about painting, then describe the piece of art that helped you change the way you saw the world.

Don't forget to address the last part of the question: "What did you do to act upon your new thinking and what have you done to prepare yourself for further study in this area?" Think about what that means. How have you changed your behavior? Have you become more active in the arts, or have you become more aware of your surroundings – or something even less obvious? In any case, do not ever neglect to answer a portion of the prompt. You need a thorough, compelling response to demonstrate your commitment to the arts.

Essay S

There may be personal information that you want considered as part of your admissions application. Write an essay describing that information. You might include exceptional hardships, challenges, or opportunities that have shaped or impacted your abilities or academic credentials, personal responsibilities, exceptional achievements or talents, educational goals, or ways in which you might contribute to an institution committed to creating a diverse learning environment.

This topic is NOT on ApplyTexas. It's a UT essay to describe special circumstances in your life. Sometimes, a student feel like he or she has managed to address the major obstacle in his or her life in Essay B. However, there may be other concerns that can only be discussed in Essay S, like something exceptionally hard that didn't necessarily get resolved.

> As much as it stinks, some problems linger, and the "what skills did you use to resolve" the problem portion of Essay B's topic simply doesn't apply. That may be a time to call upon Essay S.
>
> Additionally, Essay S is a remarkable place to discuss a talent or commitment that sets you apart from your peers. UT wants an environment that encourages thought and a growth in collective understanding. As someone with an extraordinary talent, hobby, or passion, you can add a unique dimension to a new graduating class at UT. This is the place to describe your obsession with magic tricks or your interest in debate. It's the opportunity to explain that even as a science major, you want to try out for a dance team, or that you write poetreven though you want to eventually study Sport Management. This is the place to describe how you are like no one else.

It's only available to UT applicants, and you can only send in Essay S after you've submitted your application. Like your résumé, you upload Essay S through the UT MyStatus page.

LETTERS OF RECOMMENDATION

Letters of recommendation can rarely sway an admissions committee, but they can be helpful in corroborating your character. That said, I encourage you to submit one or two letters of recommendation to UT.

First, you should ask your teachers in person if they are comfortable writing letters on your behalf. Give them copies of your résumé and your favorite essay. Second, you should send them a request through the UT MyStatus page. You don't have to give them envelopes for UT because they can easily submit everything online.

SUPPLEMENTAL INFORMATION FORM

Let me shout something loudly and clearly: "Check your MyStatus page after you've applied!!!" I had a student just this year who never looked at MyStatus, and he never wound up submitting the Supplemental Information Form. This document is literally a no-brainer. It lets you give the University information about the courses you've taken in high school, and it provides some preliminary financial information to the University. It does not substitute for a transcript or a FAFSA (financial aid application). However, if you fail to submit the Supplemental Information Form, your application will not be considered. Please do it. Don't be silly.

16

HONORS PROGRAMS

There are multiple opportunities to join honors programs at UT, even after you've started at the University. However, I am going to give you an overarching introduction to the honors programs that are available to freshman applicants. Be aware that these programs are exceedingly competitive, and the admissions committees are looking for a special zing in a student, something that goes beyond grades and/or test scores. I have had students at the very top of their class who have not been accepted, and I've had students who were far less impressive numerically who have gotten in because of their demonstrated zeal for learning.

Honors programs have separate applications, through which you submit letters of recommendation, résumés, and honors essays. You need to submit those application AFTER you submit ApplyTexas. You have the opportunity to indicate on ApplyTexas if you intend to apply to an honors program, but even if you don't check that box, you can do so later.

BUSINESS HONORS PROGRAM

This is a small business program that follows an MBA model, using case-studies to analyze business models and business decisions. It's super cool and highly competitive. The students I've had matriculate into this program have had high 30s on the ACT or 2200+ on the SAT and been in the top 5% of their class.

ENGINEERING HONORS PROGRAM

This is a program that enhances the regular undergraduate experience. Unlike other honors programs, you don't have a different curriculum, but rather a set of additional opportunities. You have honors housing and honors mentors, as well as honors events. Plus, you have the chance to do an undergraduate honors thesis.

LIBERAL ARTS HONORS PROGRAM

This is a really cool program that gives its students the opportunity to delve deeply into the field of liberal arts that interests them, but it also incorporates special honors classes into students' curricula. The program offers smaller classes with excellent professors, and it encourages the development of stronger writing and analytical skills – valuable in any future profession. Furthermore, Liberal Arts Honors Students take part in internships and study abroad in their time at UT, becoming career-ready and culturally aware.

NATURAL SCIENCE HONORS PROGRAMS

In Natural Sciences, there are college-wide honors programs, but there also department-specific programs. In these programs, students take part in smaller classes, have intensive academic advising, and work on the Freshman Research Initiative. With respect to college-wide programs, there are the Dean's Scholars, the Health Science Scholars, and the Polymathic Scholars. The departmental honors programs are the Turing Scholars Programs in the Department of Computer Science and the Human Development and Family Sciences Honors Program.

Students can apply to one or more of the Natural Science honors programs, so don't feel limited. Just be prepared to tackle a research-intensive program that will open doors to an array of career opportunities you may never have considered.

PLAN II HONORS

This is the big daddy – the honors program that spawned other honors programs. Plan II is a college within a college, providing a wonderful liberal arts background that students can use to complement any degree program at UT. I have had students go in through Plan II Engineering, as well as through Plan II Liberal Arts. You should really look closely at Plan II because it's different in so many ways, and it deserves your real consideration – more than you can give by reading my cursory summary here.

17

ALTERNATIVE PATHWAYS TO UT

PACE & CAP

No matter how awesome you are, there's a chance that you won't get into UT – unless you're automatic. UT knows that qualified students get rejection letters, and the admissions people understand that some students don't find a successful academic rhythm until college. That's why the University has created different routes to UT Austin. If you really want to graduate from UT Austin, then there is a way for you to achieve that goal.

The PACE Program
Path to Admission through Co-Enrollment

PACE is a relatively new option, begun in the 2013-2014 school year. It's a coordinated, co-enrollment program between UT and Austin Community College (ACC). The way it works is that PACE programs take 3 hours each semester through the School of Undergraduate Studies and 12 hours each semester from ACC. At UT, students will start with a UT Signature Course, which you can research more on the UT page, and their second semester, PACE students can take a course that fits into their academic program. To ensure that they make good decisions, PACE students meet weekly with advisors and can receive even greater oversight than regular UT students might get.

By the end of two semesters, PACE students will have a total of 30 college credit hours. In order to matriculate as full-time UT students as sophomores, PACE students must maintain at least a 3.0 GPA at UT and a 3.2 at ACC. Generally speaking, those students will join the UT community as students in the School of Undergraduate Studies, but they have the option of applying as external transfer students to competitive schools, such as business and engineering.

What's especially nice about PACE is that you get to start off in Austin, which is college kid heaven. You get a UT ID card, you can get settled with a roommate, and you may join Greek life. However, that may NOT be the best situation for someone who has a hard time focusing. Remember, Austin is where GPAs go to die.

That brings me to the potential cons of the PACE program. As awesome as PACE is, there are some important things you should know. First, it's not available to everyone. PACE is for highly motivated students whom the University could not offer admission as entering freshmen. Acceptance to PACE should be viewed as an honor because it truly is. Second, you should know that PACE may be challenging. Some students have a hard time maintaining 15 hours their first semester of school, and you must finish 15 hours per semester to remain part of PACE. What that means is that you can't just come in through PACE and go spend every night on 6th Street. This is nose-to-the-grindstone time. Hold yourself together and excel in school. That way, you'll remain in PACE and keep your options for your future major wide open.

CAP
Coordinated Admissions Program

This is a tried-and-true program at UT that starts students off at a satellite campus, such as UT San Antonio, UT Tyler, UT Permian Basin, etc. Like PACE, students in CAP must complete a total 30 hours over the course of two 15-hour semesters. CAP students must maintain a minimum GPA of 3.2.

CAP students get excellent advising and have a clear set of first-year courses to take, and each school provides an exhaustive list of approved courses for transfer. Don't take classes that aren't on that list!

They also provide you with a list of suggested courses, based upon your goals at UT Austin, so that you eventually have the option of majoring in any one of UT's degrees.

It's important for you to understand that UT only guarantees CAP students entry into the School of Undergraduate Studies, College of Liberal Arts, or College of Natural Sciences. For other colleges, such as Engineering or Business, you will have to apply in a competitive transfer pool. Now, you should be able to focus during your time in CAP. You won't be in Austin, and your entire mission for that first year will be pulling out the best GPA of your life. If your mind ever drifts to anything else, remind yourself of your purpose.

Students' main complaints about CAP are that they can't pledge a fraternity or sorority during freshman year. Frankly, I can't get all worked up about that; you can pledge as a sophomore. Furthermore, if your main goal is to graduate from UT Austin, then you really can't afford the luxury of Greek social life. I have helped countless students who are applying to grad school who look back on their first year of college and cringe. They are still trying to explain those grades away...but they never can. You live with your college transcript for the rest of your life. With that in mind, take your first-year classes seriously and lay a solid foundation for your future.

If you're in CAP, just work hard and save your play for the holidays. Like Mr. Washington explained, UT offers every student an avenue to get there and graduate from there. CAP may be your ideal chance to get on that road.

AFTERWORD

I hope I've given you some useful words of guidance here. In the future, I intend to add to this book and release updated editions. After all, UT changes every year, so we must do our best to keep up.

There are also many special programs that we would like to cover, and we will send updates via email to people who sign up for our newsletter through our website.

I know the process may still seem overwhelming, and that's because it's so hard to control and predict. The best you can do is try to chart a course that reveals your goals and your talents. As I've said in this book in many places, if you want to graduate from UT, there IS a way for you to reach that goal. It may not be the direct path you're dreaming of, but all's well that ends well.

If there's anything I've learned from writing this book, it's that the people at UT are more than happy to answer questions. They are not out to reject people. They're real people, whose overarching goal is to abide by fair practices.

I wish you all the best in your pursuits, and I thank you so much for reading this material. I hope it wasn't too dry!

18

NOT DISCUSSING FINANCIAL AID

I know that many families have questions about how to pay for college, but that's not my area of expertise. I encourage you to call the financial aid office and to research school-based scholarships. I don't think you should bite off more financial burden than you can chew, so if you're feeling nervous about the cost of attending UT for four years, then you should make use of your local community college. No one will ever see on your diploma whether or not you started at community college; they only see where you finish. Don't fall into debt over pride.

That's really all I can offer because I want to stick to topics that I actually know. Financial aid is its own animal, and the only thing I know with absolute certainty is that you need to minimize your debt. Check out all options before taking out loans!

ENDNOTES

[1] Here's the way it actually works: SB 175 is Texast legislation that says that universities in Texas must fill up to 75% of their class with the top ten percent of the graduating classes at all Texas high schools. At UT, the percentage gaining automatic admission has shrunk because they fill the class more rapidly. If UT took all top ten percent, they would have nothing but top ten percent students in the entire entering freshman class. What this means is that the legislation hasn't changed, but the school can only offer space to the top seven percent.

[2] http://www.utexas.edu/graduation-rates/

[3] I pulled this from the UT Admissions page, and I want you to go directly to the page because it's possible for these numbers to change. As of the publication of this book, the UT website was updated last in July 2013; it could easily change. http://bealonghorn.utexas.edu/freshmen/admission/majors/engineering

[4] Bureau of Labor Statistics (www.bls.gov)

[5] Money.cnn.com/pf/best-jobs

[6] UT Chemical Engineering webpage

[7] Bureau of Labor Statistics (www.bls.gov)

[8] www.caee.utexas.edu/ceareasofpractice/index.cfm

[9] I first read about the proposed invisibility cloak last summer, but it's real news now! "Researchers Design First Battery-Powered Invisibility Cloak." UT News. The University of Texas at Austin, 18 Dec. 2013. Web. 21 Apr. 2014. <http://www.utexas.edu/news/2013/12/18/cloaking-device-ut-research/>.

[10] Taken directly from the University of Texas' Petroleum and Geosystems Engineering page for future freshmen. http://www.pge.utexas.edu/future/undergraduate

[11] http://journalism.utexas.edu/undergraduate/curriculum

[12] http://moody.utexas.edu/sites/communication.utexas.edu/files/attachments/osa/CMS-Fact-Sheet.pdf

[13] http://www.com.washington.edu/undergraduate-students/communication-career-paths/human-relations-management/

[14] http://www.edb.utexas.edu/education/assets/files/ci/utut/AboutUTUT_4-4.pdf

[15] http://www.tasb.org/services/hr_services/salary_surveys/documents/tchr_highlights_landing.pdf

[16] http://latino.foxnews.com/latino/politics/2013/08/07/nearly-38-million-in-us-speak-spanish-at-home-census-says/

[17] http://www.tasb.org/services/hr_services/salary_surveys/documents/tchr_highlights_landing.pdf

[18] https://www.edb.utexas.edu/atep/faq2.htm

[19] Interview with Brian Farr, February 28, 2014.

[20] http://www.glassdoor.com/Salaries/physical-education-teacher-salary-SRCH_KO0,26.htm

[21] http://www.glassdoor.com/Salaries/geophysicist-salary-SRCH_KO0,12.htm

[22] http://www.glassdoor.com/Salaries/hydrogeologist-salary-SRCH_KO0,14.htm

[23] http://www.tasb.org/services/hr_services/salary_surveys/documents/tchr_highlights_landing.pdf

[24] http://blogs.wsj.com/atwork/2013/04/29/and-the-highest-paid-college-majors-are/

[25] Tesfaye, Casey, and Patrick Mulvey, comps. "MCAT, LSAT, and Physics Bachelor's." *American Institute of Physics*: Focus on (December 2013): n. pag. Dec. 2013. Web. 22 Apr. 2014. <www.aip.org/statistics>.

[26] https://www.utexas.edu/cola/depts/philosophy/

[27] http://www.utexas.edu/cola/depts/government/about/Overview.php

[28] http://cns.utexas.edu/about/departments/computer-science

[29] "Enrollment by College, Department, and Level." *University of Texas Office of Information Management*. University of Texas at Austin, n.d. Web. 20 Jan. 2014.

[30] Fisher, Kristi D. "FINAL Enrollment Analysis for Fall 2013." Letter to University of Texas President William Powers, Jr. 1 Nov. 2013. University of Texas Office of Information Management. University of Texas at Austin, 1 Nov. 2013. Web. 20 Jan. 2014.

[31] Confirmed by the Office of Information Management and Analysis. 24 April 2014.

[32] "University of Southern California." College Navigator. National Center for Education Statistics, 2013. Web. 28 Apr. 2014.

[33] "University of Texas at Austin." College Navigator. National Center for Education Statistics, 2013. Web. 28 Apr. 2014.

[34] "Application/Admission/Enrollment Information for First-Time Freshmen by Ethnicity/Race." University of Texas Office of Information Management. University of Texas at Austin, n.d. Web. 20 Jan. 2014. <https://sp.austin.utexas.edu/sites/ut/rpt/Documents/IMA_S_AppAdmitFTIC_2013_Fall.pdf>.

[35] Fisher, Kristi D. "FINAL Enrollment Analysis for Fall 2013." Letter to University of Texas President William Powers, Jr. 1 Nov. 2013. University of Texas Office of Information Management. University of Texas at Austin, 1 Nov. 2013. Web. 20 Jan. 2014.

[36] Ibid.

[37] These numbers are standard throughout Texas, but I got the figures word-for-word from the UT website: "Texas Success Initiative: Exemptions." University of Texas School of Undergraduate Studies. University of Texas at Austin, n.d. Web. 21 Apr. 2014. <http://www.utexas.edu/ugs/tsi/exemptions>.

DISCLAIMER

Although the author sought and received helpful information from a variety of sources in connection with writing this book, including people employed by UT, current and former contractors with UT, current and former students of UT, and a host of others with personal knowledge of UT's practices, this work is wholly that of the author. Neither UT, nor any of the UT-related or other people consulted, is responsible for any of the content.

Made in the USA
Lexington, KY
22 May 2014